TIBET

TIB

A book by
Jugoslovenska Revija, Belgrade
and the Shanghai People's Art Publishing House

Authors:
Ngapo Ngawang Jigmei
Khrili Chodra
Chapel Tsetan Phuntso
Na Zhen
Cai Xiansheng
Jampei Chinlei
Dongge Luosantselie

Design by:
Massimo Vignelli

With a Preface by Harrison Salisbury

McGraw-Hill Book Company
New York, San Francisco, St. Louis

Library of Congress
Catalog Card Number:
DS 786.T493 951.505 81-8178

First published
in the U.S. 1981 by
McGraw-Hill Book Company

ISBN 0-07-032538-3

Director and Editor-in-Chief
Nebojša Tomašević

Edition Editors:
Chang Chun
Pan Shicong
Yang Kelin

Special Editors:
Khrili Chodra
Cai Xiansheng

Translations by:
Liu Shengqi
Lo Chaotien
Yang Zhihong
Ren Zhiji

Produced by Scala

This book was produced in
cooperation with the Shanghai
People's Art Publishing House,
Shanghai

Director and Editor-in-Chief
Li Huaizhi

Photographs by:
Yang Kelin
Xie Xingfa
Gu Shoukang
Dai Jiming
Yang Minghui
Zhang Hanyi
Cai Long
Wu Fuqiang
Ren Shiyin
Yin Hong
Liu Qiangang
Liu Tiesheng
Traggoluo
Jia Mingzu
Xu Zhenshi
Shao Hua An
Gao Guorong
Gao Shenkang

Printed in Milan, Italy by
Amilcare Pizzi Arti Grafiche, S.p.A.
for McGraw-Hill Book Company
1221 Avenue of the Americas
New York, N.Y. 10020
Bound in Switzerland

Contents

Preface

No land has so captured man's imagination for its remote particularity and its almost mystical aura than Tibet, the hidden kingdom in the heart of Asia, the roof of the world.

Tibet's apartness has persisted to the present day. The age of the steam locomotive passed Lhasa by. There is no rail connection to this jewel in the lotus, no railroad that approaches within hundreds of miles of Tibet's forbidding frontiers. Only with the coming of the People's Republic of China has Tibet been linked to the outer world by extremely rugged highways, often impassible in the monsoon season, built at the cost of several hundred lives. Airplane service is limited. There are so few places a plane can land.

Despite impressive obstacles of geography and geology Tibet, now a part of the People's Republic of China, is slowly beginning to strengthen contacts with the outer world. A few tourists each year are now permitted to enter the still almost forbidden kingdom. Trade with Nepal over the Chinese built highway which links Katmandu and Lhasa is slowly growing. Travelling along this rock-cleft engineering marvel in 1980 I encountered the first stages of travel by Tibetans in and out of their country in two decades and the almost lively movement of the Nepalese traders across the frontier. Chinese planes now fly from Chengdu, capital of Sichuan province, to Tibet's civil airport 130 kilometers from Lhasa several times a week.

It is more than twenty years since the Dalai Lama fled Lhasa in 1959 and the People's Liberation Army marched in and established Communist rule in this ancient theocracy replacing the Buddhist priesthood installed in the forbidding heights of the great Potala, residence of Buddhist incarnations for some 300 years.

The decades of Communist rule after 1959 were not a happy time for Tibet. It suffered catastrophic outrages during the so-called Cultural Revolution of the rule of the Gang of Four headed by Chiang Ching, the wife of Mao Zedong. Thousands of Tibetans were in prisons, tortured, executed or died in forced labor camps. The great temples and monasteries of Yellow Buddhism were closed. Many were gutted and destroyed by fanatical red guards, youthful extremists, both Chinese and Tibetan. Religious frescoes were mutilated. Jewel-studded objects of gold and silver were wrenched from altars. Priests were slaughtered, worship forbidden.

The country's economy historically based on nomadic herding of sheep, yaks and goats and the cultivation of barley, rape, and millet in high upland fields was wrecked. Public health deteriorated.

Chinese cadres supported by the P.L.A. and aided by Tibetan sympathizers ruled Tibet. Only in 1979 and 1980 did all this change. The Chinese brought their disastrous program to an end. Today Tibet is beginning to live again. Monasteries and temples have reopened, many still in a sad state. Some never can be restored. Priests, in greatly reduced numbers, again inhabit some of the monasteries and tend to yak butter lamps before the altars. Barriers to public worship are being removed. The shrines are crowded with pilgrims who walk hundreds of miles prostrating themselves every six feet of the stone trails, to make their obeisance.

Two-thirds of the Chinese cadres are being sent back to China and their functions turned over to Tibetans. All Chinese who remain in Tibet must learn the language. Private business, private property, private ownership, private farming and animal husbandry have been restored. Taxes are being remitted in an effort to restore the economy. Ill-advised schemes to grow rice and wheat in Tibet's high altitudes have been abandoned and Tibet has been given back to the yak, the sheep and the goat. The network of schools is being established as well as higher education institutions. New emphasis is being given to public health.

The Chinese led by Party Secretary, Wu Yaobang, have laid down a new policy for Tibet. If it is not quite Tibet-for-the Tibetans it is still far different from Tibet-for-the Chinese. China's mistakes in Tibet have been openly acknowledged and Chinese officials make no secret of their hope for reconciliation with the Dalai Lama. They hope for his return to his native land from India where he took refuge in 1959.

In 1979 and 1980, four major delegations of Tibetans representing the Dalai Lama came to Tibet for lengthy travel, two led by brothers of the Dalai, one by his sister and the fourth by young Tibetan exiles from five different countries. The visitors spent as long as six months in travelling about Tibet. It would be wrong to say that they were not saddened by what they saw. The years since 1959 have taken a heavy toll on Tibet. Lhasa, always a primitive city, has lost much of its charm due to the deterioration of buildings, the destruction of holy places, and the decline of street life, a depressed state of the populus. Tales of horror experienced by many Tibetans under Chinese rule shocked the Tibetans-in-exile.

Tibet and China historically have never had a close or warm relationship. Tibet has been subject to Chinese suzerainty when Beijing is strong; has been more or less independent when China is weak. In the deep past, Tibet even conquered western areas of China. Remote Tibet surrounded by great countries has always tried to play a balancing game. Sometimes between the empires of Russia and England, sometimes between India and Communist China with Soviet Russia watching across the mountain ranges.

Tibet's status is that of an autonomous region within the Chinese People's Republic. Beijing has suggested a willingness to place domestic affairs in the hands of the Dalai Lama if he is willing to renounce independence and let China handle foreign relations and defense. But both sides are wary; if the Dalai Lama comes back, would not China try to turn him into a powerless puppet? In Bejing some ask: if the Dalai returns would he not plot with India or Russia and again raise the banner of an independent Tibet?

For millennia Tibet depended on high mountain walls for isolation and a fierce national spirit to preserve her way of life and of religion. No longer is that isolation complete.

Small wonder that Tibet's future is hard to predict. But one thing is certain. Whatever happens the essential uniqueness of these people of Shangri La, their marvelous mystique, will not readily be changed and the majesty and beauty of Tibet's mountains and deserts will persist to eternity.

Harrison Salisbury

5

Chapter I   Tibet Past and Present: An Introduction

Ngapo Ngawang Jigmei

1. *Mount Chomolungma (Everest). This photo was taken from a height of 16,500 feet above sea level at a distance of 31 miles from the peak.*

2. *A Tibetan face.*

3. *The Potala Palace in Lhasa, capital of Tibet. It was the sacred residence of the Dalai Lama.*

4. *A fresco showing Princess Wen Cheng, the figure sitting sideways in the cart, coming to Tibet.*

5. *Tibetans worshiping.*

People have for centuries thought of Tibet as a land mysterious and remote, as a wilderness perpetually covered with ice and snow or else as a kind of fairyland—a latter-day Eden like the Shangri-la of James Hilton's novel *Lost Horizon,* a place far removed from the cares and troubles of the world. There have been countless descriptions of Tibet, some genuine and others purely imaginary, and the useful though by no means exhaustive bibliography at the end of this book will provide some idea of the curiosity which our country has always excited.

But I have always hoped that there might be a comprehensive account of Tibet that would give people a vivid understanding of our land as it really is.

Now this book is just such a work, a faithful record of real life in present-day Tibet. The photographers suffered considerable hardships in taking pictures of our snow-capped mountains, rivers, lakes, towns and villages, monasteries, local customs and daily life. The reader and viewer will be rewarded with a genuine idea of our landscape, the life of our towns, and the detailed and significant work of our artists. We might call this book a miniature of Tibetan life that has the beauty of a drop of water reflecting the "the seven colors of the sun."

For those readers who have actually visited Tibet, the book may I hope serve as an informative reminder of what they saw here and what they felt about it. To the others who have never been to our land it may give such an impression of this "roof of the world" that they may some day come mountaineering or sightseeing or exploring here. In short, it is my hope that this publication will help to turn memories and curiosity into knowledge and understanding, and encourage people to come to Tibet and see for themselves.

With this end in view, as a Tibetan I take the greatest pleasure in introducing the reader to the history, culture, sights, and customs of Tibet, and to the joys and sorrows that our land has enjoyed and endured in its long history. I cannot think that there is a reader who does not have something to gain from this encounter. For in the words of the thirteenth-century Tibetan poet, scholar, and Buddhist leader Sakya Pandita,

> The ocean does not resent too much water,
> Nor does the treasury resent too much treasure.
> The people do not resent too much wealth,
> And the wise do not resent too much knowledge.

When we speak of Tibetan history, we naturally think first of the well-known legend that the Tibetan race is descended from the union of a macaque monkey and an ogress. This is a story that has come down through the centuries, developed and enriched in poetry, in many classic historical works, and in wall painting. It is described most minutely in the *Mirror of the Royal Genealogy of Tibet* (1388) by the historian Sonam Gyamtschen. According to him, "Tibet was originally the place where the ogress of the rocks ran amok. There were no human beings then. Avalokitesvara—an exalted deity known as the Bodhisattva of Mercy and called Chenresi by the Tibetans—sent another deity transformed into a macaque down into the world to relieve the distress of the living creatures there. The macaque had union with the ogress, and six little monkeys were born to them. These multiplied and becaoe 500 monkeys. They ate of the fruits of the trees and of wild grain, so in the course of time their tails became short and they learned to speak and turned into human beings, the ancestors of the Tibetans. At that time the mountains were covered with forests; water streamed from the crevices of Mount Sumeru and ran in all the valleys, and highland barley, wheat, beans, and buckwheat were abundant. So they tilled the land and built cities and a king of Tibet emerged, creating the distinction between a sovereign and his subjects."

Through the mists of history we may discern in this story the vague recollections and traditions of a people in remote antiquity seeking for some way of expressing their life and their labors.

By about 100 B.C. agriculture was an established fact and, as Sonam Gyamtschen wrote, people knew "how to make plough and yoke by drilling holes in wood, how to make two oxen till the land by shouldering a pole, how to turn the plain into farmland and divert water into canals." In addition, our remote ancestors made at least one original contribution to the art of domesticating animals and rearing them for meat and for work in the fields. They created a new strain by crossbreeding: the dzo, the offspring of a cow and a yak. The yak is probably the earliest domesticated animal known to the Tibetans, and its name is native Tibetan, though it has passed into most Western languages. The yak itself is well adapted to the cold and lack of oxygen of high Tibet, but the dzo is even better suited to this climate.

The development of agriculture was based largely on stock breeding, the introduction of new types of seed, and the improvement of the irrigation system. According to an ancient folk legend, credit for obtaining the seeds of the hardy highland barley known as gingke, the staple food of Tibet, belongs partly to man's friend the dog. An ancient Tibetan prince put on a dogskin cape and went and stole the seeds from the supernatural "Riwuda, king of the mountain." The prince hid the seeds in the tail of his cape, returned to the world, and brought the seeds back to his people. The fact that this ancient legend is still current among the peasants of Tibet shows how much the gift of these seeds is valued and held in reverence.

Since time immemorial Tibet has had a system of irrigation adapted to natural conditions. We can still see the remains of ancient irrigation canals beside the Yarlung Tsangpo River in the Lhoka region of Tibet. In recent years irrigation has proceeded apace. A great deal of arid land has now been irrigated, and the vast sweeps of the Tibetan countryside are studded with small-scale power stations built on canals.

Elementary astronomy came into being independently in Tibet as the servant of early agriculture. In order to gain an understanding of the climate and seasonal changes and so find the proper times for ploughing, sowing, and harvesting, Tibet's farmers made basic discoveries in this science and worked out their own method of recording years, months, days, and hours. With the diffusion of the Chinese calendar—involving a sixty-year cycle, the two opposing dark, feminine and light, masculine principles of Yin and Yang, and the five elements of fire, earth, iron, water, and wood—the Tibetan calendar was greatly improved and elaborated. This scientific milestone was first recorded in the *Depter Marpo* (Red History) in 1346 and is mentioned in other early historical works. After the introduction of Buddhism in the seventh century the Indian calendar system also came into use, and a fusion of the old and the new eventually, in the eleventh century, resulted in the Tibetan calendar that is still in use today. It is a lunar calendar but also numbers 360 days a year, so that some days must be omitted to make it correspond to the moon's waxing and waning. Differences from the solar calendar are compensated for by the insertion of extra months every nineteen years. The calendar has sixty-year cycles in which the twelve zodiacal animals—mouse, bull, tiger, hare, dragon, snake, horse, sheep, monkey, bird, dog, and pig—are combined with the five elements to distinguish the year. Each of the elements is used alternately in its masculine and its feminine aspect. We are now in the (male) iron-bird year of the sixteenth cycle. We can see from all this that Tibetans have long been able to appreciate and adapt the achievements of others—and as Sakya Pandita said,

> If it is good advice,
> One should listen to the words of a child.
> If you can obtain spice from it,
> The navel of a wild beast is desirable.

Tibetan medicine and pharmacology emerged from much accumulated experience in fighting disease in often severe climatic conditions. In the eighth century of the Christian calendar, Tibet had an outstanding physician in Yutok Yontan Gonpo, justly considered the founder of Tibetan medicine, for his clinical experiments and experience resulted in a great system for the use of drugs that has come down to the present day. As John F. Avedon has recently pointed out, this system is a mixture of herbal cures and Buddhist practice, first described in four medical Tantras—treatises showing "the way." These were introduced into Tibet in the eighth century, and their 1,400 pages today can still be recited verbatim by eminent practitioners of the medical art. They delineate 84,000 diseases grouped into 1,004 separate categories, for which 2,000 mixtures of herbs and minerals are listed as remedies. Hundreds of subsequent commentaries supplement the Tantras, which attribute all illness to imbalances among the three humors that govern the human body—wind, bile, and phlegm. (See Bibliography.)

In traditional Tibetan medicine there is much use of herbs and spices and other foods. The pomegranate, for example, is fed to patients with stomach ailments. Blood letting is practiced, and hot steam baths are given. In these and other medical practices religion plays an important part; all treatment is accompanied by rites and prayers.

The Tibetans' practice of celestial burial, in which the corpse is dissected and fed to vultures so that the soul is free to depart from it, has helped doctors in their knowledge of anatomy and their understanding of the causes of death; their firsthand observation of this practice has provided a scientific basis for Tibetan medicine. Though it is true that religion and theology have made science their maidservant, medicine is held in the highest esteem, and the relief of bodily suffering, according to Buddhist doctrine, is a means to salvation. And in the course of Tibet's long history the unique features of its medicine and pharmacology have been put into practice in clinical diagnosis and effective treatment.

On Chagpori Hill opposite the Potala Palace in Lhasa there stood until recently an ancient institution called Montsi Khang (Peak House). It was here that monks and laymen were trained in Tibetan medicine, but the school also administered the astronomical almanac, by which propitious days and other important matters were determined. It was the foremost institution of higher academic learning in Tibet. Now there is a fine new hospital in the bustling city of Lhasa, complete with all the most modern equipment and techniques, and there is the recently founded Tibet Medical College, with modern medical therapeutics as its primary function; but traditional medicine has not been neglected. At present the new medicine and the traditional supplement each other in serving the people, each with its role to play; teaching, research, and treatment in both are being practiced side by side.

Buddhism came to Tibet in the seventh century of the Christian calendar, and it gradually replaced but also to some extent fused with the primitive previous local religion, called Bon, giving Tibetan Buddhism a distinctly Tibetan coloring. Practiced in Tibet by an enormous number of people for over a thousand years, with countless monasteries and a vast accumulation of sacred scripture, Buddhism has penetrated into every aspect of Tibetan culture, and there is nowhere in the country where its influence is not all-pervading. The grandiose and awe-inspiring temples reproduced in this book bear witness to the importance of religion to the Tibetan people.

The first monastery built on truly Buddhist principles, constructed around 779, rises at Samye to the south of Lhasa. It was founded by the Tibetan king Trisong Detsen (who reigned from 755 to 797) under the guidance of the famous Indian pandits Padmasambhava, known to Tibetans as Guru Rimpoche (the Precious Master), and Santarakshita. Its great hall has three stories combining the Indian, Chinese, and Tibetan architectural styles. On the four sides, surrounded by a wall, are four pagodas symbolizing "the four continents"—India, China, a mythical northern Asia, and Persia. There is also an iron-walled symbolic structure which represents Mount Meru, a mythical mountain at the center of the world. The traditional Buddhist world picture is reflected in this plan, and the architecture is magnificent and the craftsmanship superb throughout. A detailed description of just how this kind of religious place should be constructed is set down in an ancient treatise called *Bazhar*. The Samye Monastery took twelve years to complete, and the celebrations that followed lasted a whole year. With the building of this monastery began the organization of communities of monks, in Tibet called lamas, the tonsure of Tibetans for monkhood, the translation of Buddhist scriptures, and the spread of Buddhism throughout the land.

Three of the greatest monasteries of Tibet date from the early fifteenth century—Gandan (1409), Drepung (1416), and Sera (1419). These have been the three monasteries of the Gelug-pa sect of Tibetan Buddhists, "the Yellow Sect," from which have come the spiritual and temporal rulers of Tibet called from which have come the spiritual and temporal rulers of Tibet called the Dalai Lamas. Gandan, to our great loss, was destroyed during the ten years' ravage of the cultural revolution, but the other two remain more or less intact, preserving the dignity and magnificence of former days. The fourth great monastery of the Yellow Sect is called Trashilungpo and was built in 1447. The traditional residence of the exalted Panchen Lama, it is situated in Shigatse, the second largest city of Tibet.

These and the other great religious places of Tibet add to the beauty of cities and mountain forests and adorn the tranquil land. In contrast to the mansions of the aristocracy and impressive government buildings, they are open to all. People enter them freely, burn incense, pray, and sightsee. They are often perched upon lofty heights; some of their buildings are enriched by huge verandas; some have convex windows; there are sometimes rows of pagodas and golden roofs. With the ringing of morning bells, the beating of drums, and the chanting of Buddhist scriptures like the wind sighing in the pines, one cannot help being struck by their peaceful and serene atmosphere. Inside, the majestic frescoes and spectacular works of sculpture bear witness to the abundant talent of Tibetan artists. The treasures in the Potala Palace, former residence of the Dalai Lama, and those in the Tsulhakhang (or Jokhang) Temple in Lhasa are the finest of all. I shall mention three frescoes of outstanding historical and artistic interest:

"The Entry into Tibet of Princess Wen Cheng for Her Marriage." Wen Cheng, from China, and Bkrikuti Devi, a Nepalese princess, both pious Buddhists, married King Songtsen Gampo (618–649) and introduced Buddhism into Tibet. Princess Wen Cheng was a figure of high prestige and great influence. She was a young and delicate girl, but as a princess from the court of the Tang dynasty her lot was to be given in marriage to the ruler of a strange and distant land—a marriage of state whose significance far exceeded matrimony. The painting depicts the arrival of Princess Wen Cheng in Lhasa in 641. The artist chose that moment to describe the grand occasion of the marriage—the carriage and guard of honor in the street, the costumes and uniforms, music and dancing and acrobatics, the bustling crowd giving a warm welcome. The excitement, hubbub, and enthusiasm as well as the solemnity of the occasion are apparent. The atmosphere of extreme gaiety makes one think of the folksong in welcome of Princess Wen Cheng that has been handed down to the present day:

> On the fifteenth day of the first month,
> When the Princess consents to come to Tibet,
> No one is afraid of the vast sandbars,
> And there are a hundred steeds to meet you.
> No one is afraid of the snow-capped mountains,
> And there are a hundred dzos to greet you.
> No one is afraid of the surging rivers,
> And there are a hundred cowhide boats to welcome you.

In "Phagpa Lodro Gyaltsen Meeting the Mongol Leader Kublai Khan" we are presented with a mid-thirteenth-century encounter between two historical figures of great importance. The Mongols then ruled in China as a foreign power, and had attained some power over Tibet. Kublai Khan granted jurisdiction over Tibet to Phagpa, who was the high lama of the powerful Sakya sect of Tibetan Buddhist monks. This is undoubtedly an important document, bearing witness to the contacts established between Tibet and China at that relatively early date, or at least between Tibet and the Yuan (Mongolian) dynasty. As the fresco suggests, Tibet was by no means actually in a subservient position at that time, and during a century or so of Tibeto-Mongol collaboration, roughly from the mid-thirteenth century to the mid-fourteenth, the Tibetan influence was perhaps the stronger of the two. When the Yuan dynasty thereafter declined and fell, Tibet regained independence and maintained it for over 200 years.

The two political leaders are shown sitting cross-legged and sharing a meal. Around them are horses and camels at rest, and at a distance we can discern the figures of peasants working in the fields. Further embellished with mountains and trees, the scene presents Kublai, the hero out of the vast Mongolian desert, and Phagpa, the youth who represented the Tibetan people, at the apex of their careers. Their bold and heroic air cannot fail to evoke respect for their achievements.

Phagpa, incidentally, was not only a politician but also a linguist. He was entrusted by Kublai Khan with the task of elaborating a new Mongolian script based on Tibetan writing. It was later called "the Phagpa script."

The history of the Yuan dynasty records that "in the prefectures and counties of Tubo [Tibet], all officials are appointed by the Imperial Preceptor." Phagpa was the first to obtain this highest post, and to the very end of the Yuan dynasty Sakyas always took charge of the military and political affairs of Tibet, ruling over 130,000 Tibetan families. For almost 100 years of the Mongolian domination, until 1349, Tibet was ruled by a succession of twenty lamas of Sakya, and after that for eighty-six years—from 1349 to 1435—by a succession of lamas of the Phamo Drupa sect. Then there was a return to secular monarchy, which lasted until 1642, when the Fifth Dalai Lama received temporal power over the country.

"The Fifth Dalai Lama Welcomed by the Emperor Shun Zhi" records one of the great state visits of history, an event of 1652 and 1653. Ngawang Lozang Gyatso (1617–1682), the Fifth Dalai Lama, came of an aristocratic Tibetan family. Ten years after he defeated his main political opponent and acquired the leadership of Tibet, he led a huge delegation—3,000 people—to Beijing to visit the Mongolian emperor of China, Shun Zhi of the then recently established Qing, or Manchu, dynasty. The artists have provided us with a series of images recording the stages of this event, from the departure in September 1652 through the journey to the arrival and reception, with a bit of sightseeing, recreation, and even preaching thrown in. As a result of this meeting, the Fifth Dalai Lama received the courtesy title of "Overseer of the Buddhist Faith on Earth under the Great Benevolent Self-subsisting Buddha of West Heaven, All-knowing Bearer of the Thunderbolt," together with a gold seal and a gold diploma. After that time the death of every Dalai Lama was reported to the Imperial Court for the record, and the reincarnation as well as the investiture of every new Dalai Lama was recorded there. The Qing dynasty thus initiated an important link between the Tibetan and Chinese governments. But in the early Qing dynasty, established in 1644 by Mongolian conquerors, the external influences upon Tibet were more Mongolian than Chinese. The word "Dalai" is itself of Mongol origin, meaning "ocean of wisdom."

Throughout the many centuries of our history, Tibetans have had to show firmness and tenacity as well as optimism. Everyone knows that the natural conditions of the high Tibetan plateau are extremely difficult, but we have accustomed ourselves to wind, snow, and severe cold, have worked out a way of living on the plateau, and by creating Tibetan civilization have contributed to the enrichment of the cultural heritage of the world. For centuries the social structure of Tibet was feudalistic, a handful of families and the great monasteries owned all the land, and most of the population were serfs. But even in oppressive times there has been no lack of poets to celebrate, in the words of an anonymous poem from around the sixth century,

> This center of heaven,
> This core of the earth,
> This heart of the world
> Fenced round with snow.

The people have not failed to produce good poems, music, dances, and dramas to enrich their lives and our culture; and all are strongly marked with our national characteristics.

Tibetan poetry is by no means confined to the level of folklore. The *Hundred Thousand Songs* by Milarepa is Tibet's literary-religious classic and one of the masterpieces of Asian literature. A translation into English, with extremely informative notes, has been made by Garma C. C. Chang (see Bibliography). Even a partial reading of this epic of religious poetry will tell a sympathetic reader more about the Tibetan soul than any amount of description or explanation. The songs themselves, individual masterpieces of mystical poetry, are in the form of tales concerning the life of this hermit and poet (1040–1123), who has been called the greatest poet-saint in the history of Buddhism.

Though his style is intensely metaphorical, Kunga Gyaltsen (1182–1251), the leader of the Sakya sect of Tibetan Buddhists who was also known as Sakya Pandita, took the virtues of clarity, stringency, and profundity to the heights of poetic art in his *Proverbs of Sakya*. More widely known, and still to be heard on the lips of the people, are the poems of Tsangyang Gyatso (1683–1706). He was no less a personage than the Sixth Dalai Lama, though as a ruler he could scarcely match his distinguished predecessor. In fact at times he virtually laid aside his great office and roamed the capital at night as a wandering poet. His work is lyrical, worldly, and deceptively simple. Far more than the earlier poets, he wrote of everyday life in ordinary human terms:

> If I yield to the maiden's wish
> I will forfeit the rule of Buddha forever;
> If I go into the mountains to ennoble my spirit
> I will hurt the damsel's feelings.

According to tradition the bard Tangton Gyalpo (1385–1464) was the father of Tibetan drama, in which tales are acted out with singing and dancing. A repertory of eight classic Tibetan dramas, which used to be performed only in the public squares, has now found an honorable place in performances in theaters also. One of Gyalpo's dramas tells the tale of a great and generous prince who gives away to a blind man all his wealth, then his eyes, then his wife, then his daughter. But his goodness is rewarded and he gets them all back again. The play is called *Timi-Kundem.*

The *Song of Gesar* recounts the exploits of a legendary warrior king of northern Asia who was said to be a suitor of Princess Wen Cheng before she married Songtsen Gampo; it is a folk epic full of the national pride of the Tibetan people, immensely popular all over the country and sung at all festivals. The *Bardo Thödol,* or *Tibetan Book of the Dead,* an ancient guide to entrance into and behavior in the afterlife, has become a classic of Oriental literature, thanks to translations into Western languages by W. J. Evans-Wentz and Giuseppe Tucci (see Bibliography).

All these works of art bear witness to the fierce will and optimistic spirit of the Tibetan people. In addition, sympathy, friendliness, and a willingness to help one another are common characteristics of the Tibetans, and it is probable that our harsh natural and social environment has helped foster these qualities. And I think I can say that simplicity and truthfulness are qualities of which the Tibetans may be justly proud. Here are some famous lines by the poet Tsangyang Gyatso:

> Affix the small black seal
> Which cannnot speak;
> Affix the seal that knows shame and keeps promises
> Between each other's hearts.

The lines express a typical sentiment of the Tibetans. The keeping of promises far exceeds the letter of the law, and to break one's word is considered a deeply shameful thing.

It should certainly also be mentioned here that the Tibetans themselves are not the only racial group living within the borders of the country. There are Menpas, Lopas, Denpas, Sherpas, and other minorities dwelling side by side on friendly and peaceful terms.

Finally I should point out that the Tibetan people have recently crossed a barrier over a thousand years old into socialism, and it is no exaggeration to say that their life has undergone an earth-shaking change. Under the veteran revolutionary leaders things got off to a good start, but just as our country was beginning to make up for lost time at terrific speed, the ten years' ravage of the cultural revolution set in all over China, and Tibet was not excepted. Socialist reconstruction came to a standstill and much precious time was lost, while wanton and irreparable damage was done to our cultural heritage.

February 1981, in the Tibetan calendar the year of the iron-bird

Tibean Place Names

The correct naming of Tibetan places is a complex and difficult affair, and particularly today, for four different reasons:

1. Tibetan is written in a script derived from the Indian script of the seventh and eighth centuries A.D. Since then the spoken language of Tibet has changed with respect to the written, much as happened with English, except more radically. One name, for example, in Tibetan can be spelled «Rwa-Sgreng» but is pronunced «Reting» or «Rating».

2. There has never been an attempt by the Tibetans to establish a roster of official place names in the Latin script corresponding to their spoken form. Hence the names used here are those found most frequently on maps and in major works of Western literature about Tibet.

3. With the arrival of the Chinese in 1951 there was a general revision of all place names, which were then transcribed in ideograms. As with all such transcriptions, signs were used to represent a collection of sounds, without any reference to the meaning of the world.

4. For transcribing Chinese ideograms into Latin script there are several systems: two of the most widely used are Wade-Giles and Pinyin. The latter is the official system in China, and now in Tibet, but its use in Latinizing a Chinese ideogram of a Tibetan place name can considerably alter the current pronunciation of that name.

The spelling of names on the map overleaf is based partly on the usage by W.D. Shakappa in his Tibet, a Political History (Yale University Press, 1973), and in part on the usage by Prof. Giuseppe Tucci in his many works about Tibet.
Below there is an attempt to give a few examples of the place name problem by presenting a certain number of names in several of their principal forms, as the reader will encounter them in different publications.

Column 1: Most current usage, reflecting contemporary pronunciation.
Column 2: Transliteration of the written form from the Tibetan script, of Sankrit origin.
Column 3: Several variants, in common use, of the same name.
Column 4: The official Chinese names in Chinese ideograms. ([1])
Column 5: Transcription of the Chinese ideogram according to the Wade-Giles system.
Column 6: Transcription of the Chinese ideogram according to the official Chinese, Pinyin, system.

1	2	3	4	5	6
Chamdo	C'ab-mdo	———	昌都	Ch'ang-tu	Qamdo Oabdo
Chongye	P'yongs-rgyas	Chunggye Chonghye	穷结	Ch'iung-chieh	Qonggyai Qonggya Qiongjie
Gyantse	rGyal-tse	Gyangtse Gyangtze Ghyantse	江孜	Ch'ang-tu Chang-tsu Chiang-tsu	Gyangzê Gyazê
Kyirong	sKyid-grong	———	吉隆	Chi-lung	Gyirong
Lhasa	Lha-sa	Lasa	拉萨	La-sa	Lhasa
Lhatse	Lha-rtse	Lhatze	拉孜	La-tsu	Lhazê
Nedong	sNe-gdong	———	乃东	Nai-tung	Nedong
Nyalam	gNya'lam		聂拉木	Nieh-la-mu	Nyalam
Sakya	Sa-skya		萨迦	Sa-chia	Sa'gya
Shigatse	gŽis-ka-rtse	Shigatze	日喀则	Jih-k'a-tse	Xigazê
Tashilhunpo	bKra-shis-lhun-po	Trashilhünpo Tashi Lhunpo	札什伦布	Cha-shih-lun-po	Zhaxilhünbo
Tsangpo	gTsang-po	Tsang-po	藏布	Tsang-pu	Zangbo
Yarlung	Yar-klungs	———	雅鲁	Ya-lu	Yarlung
Yatung	———	———	亚东	Ya-tung	Yadong
Tibet	Bod (pron. Pö)	Thibet	西藏	Hsi-Tsang	Xizang

(1) These were written especially for this book by Prof. Takaharu Miyashita, Lecturer at the University of Florence and master calligrapher.

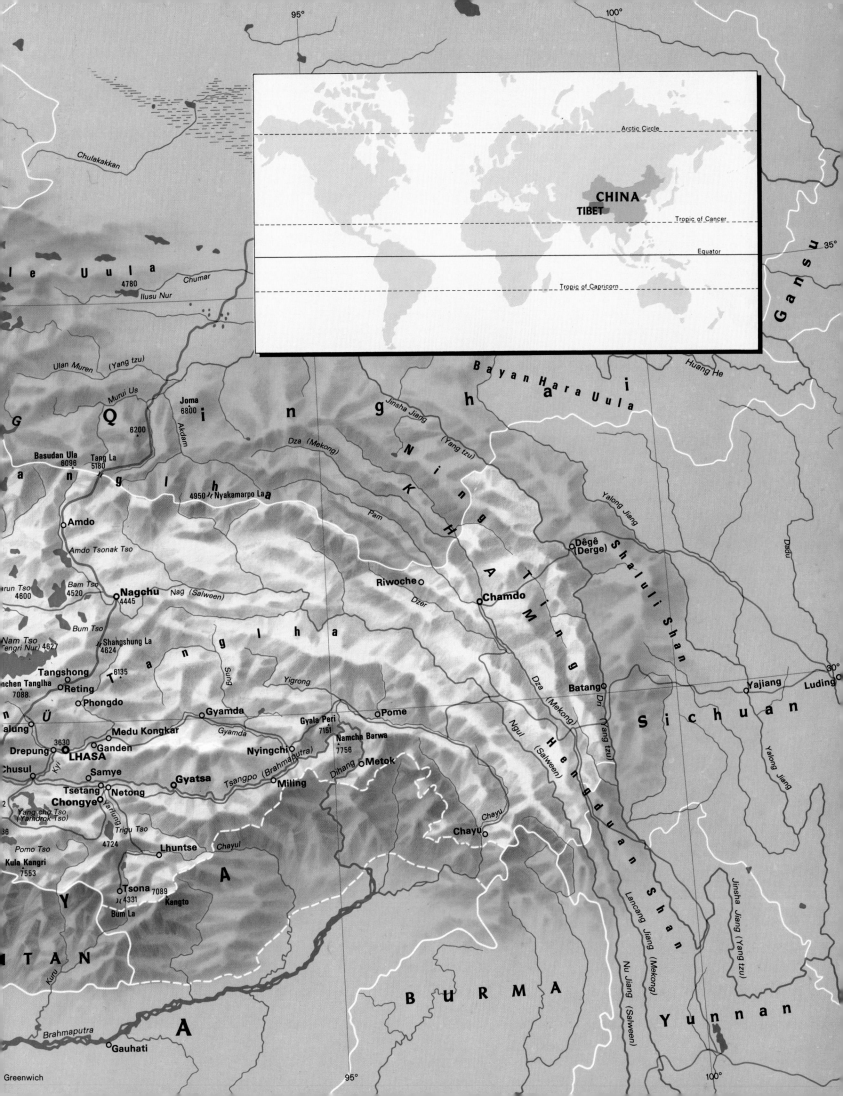

Chulakakkan

le U u l a
4780

Ilusu Nur

Chumar

95°

100°

Arctic Circle

CHINA
TIBET

Tropic of Cancer

Equator

Tropic of Capricorn

Gansu

35°

Ulan Muren (Yang tzu)

Murui Us

B a y a n   H a r a   U u l a

Huang He

Jinsha Jiang

Joma
6800

Q   i   n

g

h

a

i

Akdam

G

6200

Dza (Mekong)

Basudan Ula
6096   Tang La
5180

n

g

4950   Nyakamarpo La

l   h

a

Pam

N

i

n

g

Yalong Jiang

Amdo

Amdo Tsonak Tso

K

Dêgê
(Derge)

Shaluli shan

Dadu

arun Tso
4600

Bam Tso
4520

Nagchu
4445

Nag (Salween)

Dzer

Riwoche

H

A

Chamdo

Dza (Mekong)

Bum Tso

Nam Tso
engri Nur) 4627

Shangshung La
4624

T

n

g

l   h

a

Sung

Yigrong

T

i

n

g

Batang

Dri

Yang tzu)

Yajiang

Luding

Tangshong

6135

Ngul

Dza (Mekong)

Sichuan

30°

nchen Tanglha
7088   Reting

Phongdo

Gyamda

Gyamda

Gyala Peri
7151

Pome

H

e

Yalong Jiang

alung

Ü

Medu Kongkar

Namcha Barwa
7756

n

Jinsha Jiang (Yang tzu)

Drepung

3630

Ganden

LHASA

Nyingchi

Tsangpo (Brahmaputra)

Dihang

Metok

g

d

Chusul

Samye

Gyatsa

Miling

u

Kyi

Tsetang   Netong

a

Chayu

Chongye

arlung

Yang cho Tso
(Yamdrok Tso)

Trigu Tso

Chayul

Chayu

n

36

Pomo Tso

4724

Lhuntse

Chayul

Kula Kangri
7553

A

Tsona 7089

TAN

4331   Kangto

Bum La

Y

Lancang Jiang (Mekong)

Nu Jiang (Salween)

Brahmaputra

A

B U R M A

Y u n n a n

Gauhati

Greenwich

95°

100°

7

6. *The Yumbu Lagang near Tsethang in the Yarlung valley in central Tibet is reputed to be the earliest palace in Tibet. According to tradition, the palace was built in honor of Nyatri Tsenpo when he descended from heaven and was made king, or Tsenpo, by the people of Yarlung.*

9

8

7. The fort of Chunggye is also located in the Yarlung valley, the cradle of Tibetan civilization.

8. These mounds are the royal tombs in Chunggye where the Tsenpos from the seventh to the ninth century were buried. The ruins of nine tombs still remain about 35 feet above the ground.

9. A stone lion, five feet in height, squats near the tombs of ancient kings in the royal cemetery at Chunggye. The rough-hewn, solemn, and forbidding animal is believed to date from the beginning of the eighth century.

10. *Songtsen Gampo, the most illustrious figure in Tibetan history, was the first Tsenpo to unify Tibet under the rule of a strong and prosperous dynasty, in the early seventh century. By assimilating the more advanced culture and technology of Tang dynasty China and other neighboring areas, his rule marked a period of general prosperity and economic and cultural development.*

11. *A royal document sent to Tibet in 1375 by Emperor Tai Zu of the Ming dynasty.*

12. *This helmet preserved in the Sakya Monastery was a gift to the head of the Sakya sect in the thirteenth century.*

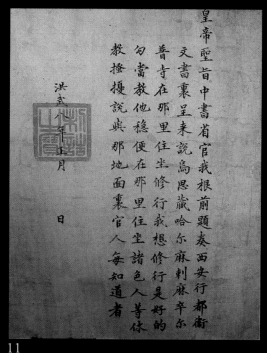

11

12

16

17

13. *A Tang dynasty painting depicting the Emperor Tai Zong (right, seated) receiving an envoy (second from left) from King Songtsen Gampo of Tibet, asking for the hand of a Tang princess.*

14. *In 1642 Gushri Khan, chief of the Qoshot Mongol tribe, called in for assistance by leaders of the Gelug-pa sect of Buddhists ("the Yellow Caps"), subdued the political power of the Karma-pa sect (divided into "Red Hats" and "Black Hats") in favor of the Fifth Dalai Lama. The photo shows the ruins of a Karma-pa monastery in Lhuntse.*

15. *A portrait of Emperor Qian Long on a Tibetan painted scroll, or thangka, and a tablet bearing the inscription "A Long, Long Life to the Emperor" in the four languages of Manchurian, Chinese, Tibetan, and Mongolian.*

16. *A Qing dynasty gold urn of 1792. When several rival candidates appeared as the reincarnation of the Dalai Lama or the Panchen Lama, the choice was decided by the drawing of lots from this urn.*

17. *Prints of the hands of the Fifth Dalai Lama on a proclamation exhorting Tibetans, monks, and laymen alike, to obey Sangye Gyatso, whom he had appointed Desi (Chief Minister) in view of his own advanced age.*

18

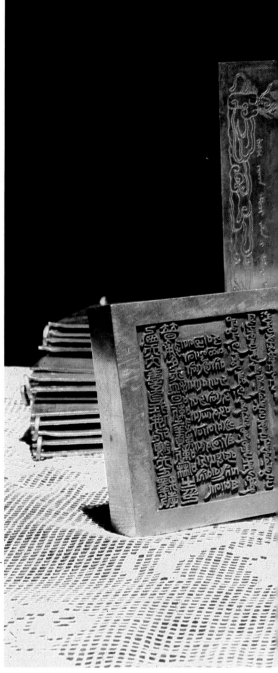

18. *A large portrait of Emperor Qian Long now preserved at the Trashilungpo Monastery in a chapel built by the Seventh Panchen Lama.*

19. *To the successive reincarnations of the Dalai Lama and the Panchen Lama gold seals and diplomas were issued. The photo shows the gold seal for the Fifth Dalai Lama, issued in 1652, and the gold diploma for the Eleventh Dalai Lama, issued in 1841.*

20

20. *The fort of Gyantse, built in 1268, the scene of heroic resistance against British troops in 1904. It is now listed as a site of national historical importance.*

21. *Spears, shields, armor, and helmets like these were used until recent times in defense of Tibetan independence, even against the modern weapons of the British in the early twentieth century.*

22. *Luding Bridge on the Dadu River once served as an important link between the Sichuan plains and the Tibetan highlands.*

23. *Lying not far southwest of Xining, the provincial capital of Qinghai, is the famous Ri Yue Shan—the Mountain of the Sun and the Moon. There is a story that when the Tang princess Wen Cheng traveled from Changan to Lhasa, she carried along a mirror in which she could see visions of her home. But on her journey she broke the mirror, which turned into the Mountain of the Sun and the Moon. When this happened, the princess gave up thinking of home and went straight on to Tibet. This stone marks the spot.*

24

24. *The sudden changes of altitude everywhere in Tibet enable one to see two seasons of the year at a single glance.*

25. *The Sichuan-Tibet Highway, with a total length of over 1,250 miles, crosses more than a dozen mountain ranges over 13,000 feet high, and is a major feat of engineering.*

26

Chapter II   The Land

Khrili Chodra

27

Ancient Tibetan legends tell us a most unlikely story—that the immensely high plateau of Tibet, surrounded as it is by the world's highest mountains, was once at the bottom of the sea. According to these legends a vast ocean inundated most of the area, while the rest was covered with primeval forests. One day five gigantic poisonous dragons came out of the sea and played havoc with the forests, stirring up such huge waves that all the vegetation was destroyed. The birds and other animals had had a premonition of this catastrophe, and now they were terrified. But just at that moment five rose-colored clouds appeared over the sea and were transformed into five fairies. They subdued the dragons, and the sea grew calm again. All the animals begged the five fairies to stay with them, and so they did. The fairies commanded the sea to withdraw and it obeyed, turning the east to rich dense forests and the west to tableland, the south to luxuriant agricultural gardens and the north to boundless grazing lands. The five fairies became the five main peaks of the Himalayas. Mount Chomolungma, known in the West as Mount Everest, is one of these five, and everyone knows it is the highest mountain in the world. The local people affectionately call it "Mount Goddess."

But unlikely as our folktale is, it has in its less fanciful details been proved by modern science to be well founded, for the Tibetan plateau was indeed part of the seabed in what geologically speaking are comparatively recent times. There have been many hypotheses as to the origins of Tibet, but in the last few decades a key to the mystery has been provided by geological and other surveys. In 1964 and 1966 investigations were made on Mount Shisha Pangma in the Himalayas and at Tulung in Nyalam County in southern Tibet. Among the findings were the fossils of two ichthyosaurs. Promptly named "the Himalayan ichthyosaurs," these animals had long pointed noses, measured 33 feet in length, and lived at the bottom of the sea 180,000,000 years ago, feeding on mollusks. This is sufficient confirmation of the fact that the Himalayas were once a sea.

In 1976 a dinosaur fossil was found near the foot of Mount Tamala in the Chamdo district in eastern Tibet. Remains of the lumbar vertebrae and teeth and ribs of the dinosaur were carefully dug out of the slopes of the mountain. As the result of tests it was calculated that the animal must have lived from 30 to 70 million years ago. The sea must have withdrawn and left behind a mountainous region, but one with plenty of lakes and watery areas. The climate must have been hot and humid, with luxuriant vegetation and so an abundance of food. Then finally the sea disappeared altogether, the lakes dried up, and what had been the bottom of the sea was pushed up higher and higher by the internal movement of the earth. In such conditions the dinosaur could no longer live, and its fossil is one sign left behind by nature in the immensely slow process of transformation. Another is that fossils of snails are to be found lying on the ground in the Himalayas. If scientists need specimens, they only have to pick them up.

There is now plenty of evidence that this hypothesis is true. Over many millions of years the mountainous plateau that is Tibet has been formed as the crust of the earth has slowly pushed and folded. And indeed, recent investigations at Mount Chomolungma show that the plateau is still rising at the rate of 0.4 to 0.8 inches a year.

26. *This fresco at the Samye Monastery shows the transformation of macaque monkeys into human beings, the legendary origin of the Tibetan race. The monastery, built in the late eighth century, is the earliest Buddhist monastery in Tibet.*

27. *This fossil of an ichthyosaur was found in Nyalam County in Southern Tibet. About 180 million years ago the Tibetan plateau was a vast expanse of sea, in which this creature reigned supreme.*

It is the largest and highest plateau on earth. Extending from 78° to 99° longitude East and from 28° to 37° latitude North, Tibet has a total surface of 460,000 square miles with an average height of 16,500 feet above the sea. It is 1,625 miles in length from west to east and 812 miles from north to south. Tibet is roughly the size of France, Belgium, Holland, Western Germany and Italy combined, or of the American states of California, Nevada, Utah, and Arizona. It borders on Kashmir, India, Nepal, Sikkim, Bhutan, and Burma to the west and south.

The mention of Tibet makes many people think of wind and snow on the high mountains. In reality the geographic features of the country are many and various and full of color. But if you visit the Tibetan plateau and wish to see towering mountains capped with eternal snows and fantastic crystal "palaces" and ice "mushrooms," you will certainly not be disappointed. To the south and west the Himalayas, the highest mountain range in the world, with a total length of over 1,500 miles, lie on the borders with India, Nepal, Sikkim, and Bhutan. The famous peaks of Mount Chomolungma, or Everest, 29,028 feet above sea level, and Mount Shisha Pangma, 26,440 feet, are the very summits of the range. The Kantisa Mountains, with an average height of 19,800 feet, lie across southwestern Tibet. The Tangla Mountains link Tibet with the Chinese province of Qinghai. They have an average height above sea level of only 14,850 feet, but as they are on the north side of Tibet, they are very cold all the year round, and contain marvelously spectacular glaciers. These ranges basically extend from east to west. The southern Hengduan mountain ranges of southeastern Tibet are exceptional in that they run in a north-south direction.

The plateau contains very extensive grasslands. The vast area of northern Tibet feeds 8 million cattle, sheep, and goats, and is one of the great grazing areas of the world. The grasslands of Tibet are in fact ideal for modern stock farming and so constitute one of Tibet's many potential resources.

Some of the rivers of the plateau flow at the highest altitudes of any in the world. The Yarlung Tsangpo River, which in India becomes the Brahmaputra, rises at the northern foot of the Himalayas at an altitude of 17,500 feet, flows eastward, turns sharply south and pierces the mountains, then takes another turn toward the west and flows into the Bay of Bengal after a total course of 1,117 miles. Three more of the great rivers of Asia—the Changjiang (Yangtze), Lancangjiang (Mekong), and Nujiang (Salween)—rise in the eastern highlands of Tibet and cut deep valleys as they flow through the eastern part of the country in a southeasterly direction. The four great lakes of the plateau are Nam Tso, Yamdrok Tso, Zilling Tso, and Mapham. They abound in fish and are surrounded by excellent grazing land.

The forests of Tibet make the country the second largest woodland area under the jurisdiction of the Chinese government. Clearly the economic importance of the woodlands is far greater in proportion than the surface they cover, 5 percent of Tibet. Besides high-mountain conifers, there are also trees typical of the southern Himalayan forest. In Chayu, Miling, and Meito counties more than 90 percent of the area is densely wooded.

These enormous forests are a boon to wildlife, including tigers, leopards, bears, orangutans, wild oxen, wild horses, monkeys, lynx, antelope, foxes, wolves, and deer, including musk deer and river deer. Forest animals supply rare medical products such as musk, pilose antler, and bear's gall, which are of great economic value. Among the plants which have commercial value are Chinese angelica, the rhizome of Chinese goldthread, rhubarb, and peppermint.

The grainlands of southern Tibet and the Changjiang, Lancangjiang, and Nujiang River valleys are the main agricultural districts, produce highland gingke barley, wheat, peas, corn, millet, potatoes, and rapeseed. Rice, peanuts, tea, tobacco, walnuts, and pepper grow in the Meito and Chayu areas. Apples, peaches, oranges, bananas, pears, and watermelons are crops introduced into Tibet during the last twenty years and now on the increase. More than forty different kinds of vegetables can be grown in the Lhasa area and around Shigatse, and many cultural and educational institutions, as well as factories and mines, are self-sufficient in the supply of vegetables.

Surveys carried out in recent years of the mineral deposits of Tibet have revealed a wealth of both ferrous and nonferrous metals, as well as nonmetallic deposits. The biggest potential copper mine in Asia lies buried in Tibet. Also present in varying quantities are iron, magnesium, chromium, zinc, antimomy, mercury, coal, oil shale, arsenic, vitriol, borax, graphite, azurite, crystal, sulfur, mirabilite, mica, barite, and talcum.

Hydroelectric power is an important resource, as Tibet is so mountainous and much of the terrain so steep that many rivers have enormous drops in altitude. The potential power to be obtained from the rivers and lakes of Tibet constitutes one-fifth of all the water resources in Chinese territory. Small-scale hydroelectric plants are now being built all over the country.

Tibet also is particularly fortunate in possessing the great natural resource of terrestrial heat. The Yangbacjin terrestrial-heat power station is already in production, generating electricity on a small scale from damp steam. Hot-water springs are also a source of natural wealth. There are many hot-water springs in Tibet, and recently their potential has been taken into consideration and even to a small extent harnessed for the production of energy and heating. They are also valuable for their curative properties, and are used for irrigation. Terrestrial heat in some form is found all over Tibet, and in the Ngari district in western Tibet there are forty-five surface indications of it.

The huge barrier of the Himalayas captures almost all the rainfall coming from the Indian Ocean. This creates a dramatic contrast between the southern part of the range where the heavy rainfalls of the monsoon create tropical forests that extend all the way to the snowline and the northern slopes of the upper range with its dry, thin air where glaciers are fed only with small summer rains and slight snowfall. The altitude of central Tibet means that the weather is generally quite cold; however, the dryness of the air and the strength of the sun during the day (because of the subtropical latitude) create rapid, even violent changes in temperature. In Chang T'ang, the highest zone of the inner plateau (15,000 to 18,000 feet), the average temperature in the hottest months is 39° to 50° Fahrenheit, with a maximum of 77° during the day and a minimum falling below freezing. The winters are fiercely cold, with average temperatures in the coldest months of 14° to 5° and with absolute minimums of around −40°. More benign conditions are to be found in the southern and eastern valleys with altitudes of less than 13,200 feet. Lhasa, at 11,900 feet, in the southern Yarlung valley, has an average temperature of 68° in July and 27° in January, and in some areas in the eastern valleys the climate is almost tropical.

The rainfall in Tibet, very scarce except in the summer months, can turn to snow at over 16,500 feet. Blizzards are common in the winter, and windstorms occur all during the year, accompanied by abrupt changes in temperature, hail, and snow.

In such climatic conditions the great southern and eastern valleys offered the best sites for settlement. They were also the most practical avenues of communication within Tibet and with the bordering regions. Therefore the majority of the Tibetan population has settled along these long natural corridors, and particularly in the great longitudinal valley of the Yarlung Tsangpo River and in the smaller valleys formed by the tributaries coming from mountain slopes.

The population of Tibet is now in the neighborhood of 1,650,000, about 3.6 persons per square mile. Ninety-six percent of the inhabitants are ethnic Tibetans; the rest are members of more than ten minority groups. The prevalent type of settlement is the small population center. The towns in Tibet usually have only a few thousand inhabitants, but manage to be economically self-sufficient. Many of the towns grew up around Buddhist monasteries. The only true city is Lhasa, the capital, with 60,000 inhabitants, on the Lhasa River, a tributary of the Yarlung Tsangpo. Another of the main centers of the Yarlung valley is Shigatse, capital of the district of the same name. In the east a notable center is Chamdo, on the river Lancangjiang and on the main road linking northern Sichuan to Tibet and continuing to the interior of the plateau and the west, crossing the whole of Tibet.

The development of other means of communication and resources will probably create a new urban hierarchy in this country, which has been isolated and immobile for centuries. This situation is mirrored in the ways of life and the traditional economic forms of Tibet. The agricultural system—practiced in zones of intensive agriculture, often terraced, in the valleys or on the slopes which are better exposed—is primitive. Tibet's flourishing breeding stocks of cattle (including the precious Tibetan yak), sheep, and goats form the most consistent resource of the traditional agropastoral economy. Aside from providing the main elements of nutrition (barley and melted butter are the two main ingredients), these stocks provide the work force for plowing and transport and primary materials such as wool and leather, which are used both for clothing and for highly appreciated handicrafts, especially carpets.

Increase in population, acquisition of new technology, and development of new lines of communication, which have not yet conquered the isolation of this stark region that is hemmed in by such imposing mountain ranges, are the conditions necessary for the full development of these resources.

Lhasa is the center of the economic development of Tibet. Here new industries, schools, and hospitals have sprung up and the members of the largest Chinese colony—mainly administrators, technocrats, and military personnel, live next to the Tibetans.

28. Khonpo Mountain near Tsethang in the Yarlung valley, according to tradition, was where the macaques changed into human beings. Tibetans therefore consider the three caves on the mountain to be the homes of their ancestors.

29. At Karo village near the town of Chamdo in eastern Tibet is the site of a Neolithic settlement of 4,600 years ago. In an area of about 2 acres large quantities of stone implements and earthenware and bone utensils have been found, as well as the bones of oxen and sheep. The design of these two earthenware pots is very similar to those of the Huanghe (Yellow River) valley of the same period.

30. The warm and fertile Yarlung valley is the birthplace of Tibetan society and the area in which the Yarlung dynasty began its rise to greatness. The historic valley includes the well-known agricultural districts of Chunggye and Neidon.

31. Mount Shisha Pangma, 26,440 feet above sea level, is one of the high peaks of the Himalayas and has a great attraction for mountaineers. It is in the Nyalam region in southern Tibet.

28

29

53

32

32. Mount Kailasa (22,156 feet) also known to Tibetans as Kang Rimpoche (Great Ice Jewel), rises alone and splendid above Manasarovar Lake and nearby pasture land in the west of Tibet. This strange towering peak with a snowy summit has been sacred since the dawn of time to Hindus, followers of the primitive Tibetan Bon religion, and Buddhists alike. A well-known hazardous pilgrimage path skirts the foot of the mountain all around.

33. A view of Mount Chomolungma (Everest), the world's highest mountain. One legend relates that it is a fairy who came down into the world but is very shy at showing her face, and indeed it is only at dawn and dusk in fine weather that the peak is visible.

33

34. In eastern Tibet, because of movements of the earth's surface, the Bayankala mountain range, the Tangla range, and the Himalayas turn abruptly southward, thereby forming the southern Hengduan ranges in southeastern Tibet and the western part of Sichuan. Thus some big rivers are forced to change their course and flow in a north-to-south direction.

35. Ice forms fantastic shapes on the high glaciers, reflecting the blue of a sky that seems very close.

36. Influenced by the hot and humid atmosphere of the Indian Ocean, the Azha glacier in the Chayu region of eastern Tibet is a high-temperature, quite mobile glacier. It melts fast and moves 1,000 to 1,300 feet a year.

35

36

37. *Scientific research on a glacier can be a risky business.*

38. *Flocks of yaks at the foot of the Himalayas.*

39. There are more than a thousand different trees in the primeval forests of Tibet, of which the most common are firs, Yunnan pines, Tibetan cypresses, and dragon spruces. Timber of various kinds is a major product of Tibet.

40

40. A cluster of giant cypresses beside the Nyang River. One of them, a tree about 172 feet in height, is over a thousand years old, so it is called "the thousand-year giant cypress."

41. *A kind of edible fungus. After the rain in summer and autumn all sorts of fungi are to be gathered in the forests.*

42. *The tremella is supposed to be good for the lungs, enriching the body fluids and nourishing the blood.*

43. *A rare species of parasitic plant. Big specimens look like a monkey's head when held in cupped hands. Hence this plant is called "monkey-head fungus."*

50. Gladiolus gandavensis. *A Tibetan variety of this well-known flower.*

51. *An* impatiens *plant, so called because its flowers burst open suddenly when touched.*

52. Hippophae rhamnoides. *One of a large family of trees growing also in Europe and Africa.*

53. *Tibetans are born horsemen, and horseracing is an important part of the festivities on New Year's Day and during other traditional festivals. Tibetan ponies have to be extremely rugged to cope with the hard terrain.*

54. *Tibetan herdsmen in the remoter areas live in tents such as these all their lives. Tents are made from yak hair woven into cloth strips about 14 inches wide, and give adequate shelter even in the coldest weather.*

55. *The Menpas of Meito have become experts at the cultivation of rice. Menpa women are here seen weeding the rice fields, wearing their characteristic straw hats that protect the back as well as the head.*

56. It may seem surprising to see banana trees in a country like Tibet, but they are grown in some quantities around Meito and Chayu in eastern Tibet, parts of which have an almost tropical climate that makes banana harvests possible for much of the year.

57. Ploughing with oxen is still the prevalent method in many parts of Tibet.

58. Southern Tibet has many fertile areas where rice, barley, and other crops flourish.

59. Lake Yamdrok Tso (Lake of Jade and Grassland) in southern Tibet. Situated 14,655 feet above sea level, it has an area of 261 square miles. The lake teems with fish, and an abundance of aquatic plants can be gathered along its shores.

61

62

60. Yaks are invaluable animals to the Tibetans. Apart from providing meat, milk, and butter, they are hardy beasts of burden, capable of long journeys through the mountains even in the worst conditions. On holidays herdsmen decorate their favorites and stage yak races.

61. The yak is a shaggy-haired breed of ox with short, strong limbs, and is adapted to the cold and the lack of oxygen of the Tibetan highlands. An average specimen weighs about 440 pounds, and has a lifespan of twenty years.

62. The yak's most important product is milk, with a yield of about a quart a day. In former times the possession of a large number of yaks was a sign of high social status.

63

64

63. *The Yarlung Tsangpo River runs eastward through Tibet before flowing into India, where it becomes the Brahmaputra. It is the world's loftiest river, rising at the northern foot of the Himalayas at a height of 17,500 feet.*

64. *To cross their rushing torrents, Tibetans have for centuries been constructing daring suspension bridges out of wild vines. This one is in the Meito district.*

65. *Another of the characteristic bridges found in many parts of Tibet. This one crosses the Yarlung Tsangpo River, which becomes extraordinarily narrow and turbulent in the stretch below Meito.*

66. *Tibet includes vast stretches of frontier, bordering on Kashmir, India, Nepal, Sikkim, Bhutan, and Burma. The militia of the various nationalities of Tibet aid national defense units in guarding the frontier.*

67

Chapter III   Customs and Rituals of the Tibetans

67. *Lhasa is still thronged with Buddhist pilgrims, who travel enormous distances on foot from such distant provinces as Sichuan, Qinghai, Gansu, and Yunnan.*

Chapel Tsetan Phuntso

Because it has always lived on a plateau more or less inaccessible to the outside world, the Tibetan nation has developed, in its long history, a series of customs and rituals quite distinct from those of other people. What follows is a brief outline of the most important of these, including ceremonies concerned with birth and death, marriage, and social behavior.

Until recently the women of Tibet had low status in society, and the treatment they received at childbirth was a sign of this. In our own times, women in the remoter pastoral areas still bear their children outside the family tent, regardless of howling wind or driving snow, because childbirth is felt to be a dirty deed; and in less backward agricultural areas childbirth may take place in cowsheds or sheep pens. Even the present Dalai Lama was born in the manger of his family's relatively prosperous farmhouse in eastern Tibet. But today more and more women are going to clinics, as they become available, or are assisted by midwives in their homes.

Then, a few days after the birth, relatives and friends come to offer their congratulations. This visit is called "bangse"—a word which means "getting rid of bad luck." According to the old scholarly tradition, this bangse ritual dates from the pre-Buddhist period of the primitive Tibetan Bon religion. In the towns people usually bring barley beer, buttered tea, and clothes for the newborn infant. As soon as guests enter the house, they present a silk khata—a finely woven piece of raw silk—to the mother and baby, pour out barley beer and tea for the mother, and pronounce a few words of blessing over the baby. In country districts, apart from barley beer and tea, visitors bring a sheepskin bag called a thangku full of tsampa—roasted, buttered barley flour—and fresh butter, symbols of their hope that the baby will grow up healthy. After pouring out the barley beer and tea for the mother, the guests put a pinch of tsampa from a grain dipper on the baby's forehead as a blessing, at the same time bestowing praises on its good looks. Banquets are given on these occasions by families rich enough to afford them.

On the morning of bangse, in out-of-the-way villages in Tibet, one can still see people making a small heap of stones outside the door of a house where a child has been born. Pine and cypress branches are then burned beside the little pile. When guests come to the house, the first thing they do is sprinkle some roasted barley flour over the stones; only then may they enter the house. In the ancient Bon religion this was an act of homage to the gods.

A month after the birth of a child, a propitious day must be chosen for the ritual of the first going out of doors. Both the mother and the infant must wear new clothes for the occasion. After visiting a temple for the mother to pray to the Buddha that the child may have a long life, they call on relatives and friends who have three generations living under the same roof, the idea being that the infant's own family may thus be helped to enjoy equal good fortune when it grows up. When a baby is first taken out of doors, a dab of soot is taken from the bottom of a pan and smeared on the tip of its nose in order to hide it from the devil. When the time comes to name the child, it is taken to some venerable elder, who is presented with a silk khata and other gifts and names the child. The names chosen often derive from the vocabulary of Buddhism—Trashi, meaning "good luck"; Tserin, "long life"; Dikyi, "happiness"; Phuntso, "satisfaction"; and so on. If the infant was born on a Thursday, it may be called Phubu, or Myima if it was a Tuesday's child. Other names of this kind are Tsechi, "the first day"; Tsegyai, "the eighth day"; and Namgang, "the thirtieth day." Some parents have their own ideas about names, such as Gorkkyai, "born to my need"; Samdru, "my dream come true"; Bukri, "a son to come"; or Chopa, "no more!" If a woman has lost many of her children, she may want the new one to be called Kyag, "dog's dung," in the hope that the devil will be put off by the name and will not snatch the child from her.

The funeral rites of the Tibetans are unusually varied and interesting. We have celestial burial, water burial, cremation, burial in the ground, and inurnment in a stupa, according to the financial and social status of the deceased and the family.

Celestial burial is used for the majority of the common people. The body of the dead person is wrapped in white cloth and kept in a corner of a room for three to five days, during which time monks come and chant scriptures so as to release the soul from the body. Friends and relatives bring a bottle of barley beer, a silk khata, some butter, a bundle of incense sticks, and sometimes a paper package containing money and labeled "condolences." The khata is for the deceased, but the money and other presents are the the family, who are not supposed to comb their hair or wash their faces or laugh or speak aloud, so that the soul of the deceased will ascend quietly. The family must also put away all the ornaments in the house. Neighbors are also expected to express grief and avoid any form of levity such as singing or dancing. A common Tibetan saying runs "If your neighbor's domestic animal dies, it is proper to grieve for three days. How much more so when it is a human being!"

A propitious day is then chosen for the funeral, which usually starts before dawn. As part of the rites the body is stripped, and the limbs are bound. The body is wrapped in a woolen blanket, called a phula, and carried by the heir to the door of the house, where the undertaker of the celestial burial is waiting to take the body away on his back.

All members of the family must attend the funeral, but only one or two close friends, representing the family, actually witness the celestial burial itself. The corpse is laid on a high rock platform, a fire is made of pine and cypress wood, and tsampa is then sprinkled on the fire. The dense smoke that rises serves as an invitation to the sacred vultures, which are never far away. The undertaker dissects the corpse from the back, cutting the flesh into small pieces, which he heaps on one side. He crushes the bones, mixes them with tsampa, and rolls this mixture into a ball; this he feeds to the vultures first, then he feeds them flesh. If any of the bone is left, it must be burned to ashes and scattered far and wide. Every morsel of the corpse must be disposed of, so that the soul is free to leave it. After the ceremony the representatives of the family produce food and barley beer, prepared in advance, for the undertaker's fee.

Water burial is chiefly used for beggars, widows and widowers, and the very poor. The corpse is taken to a river bank, dismembered, and thrown in, or it may be wrapped in white cloth and thrown in whole. When infants die, their bodies are put in porcelain jars covered with lids and thrown into the river, though sometimes these jars are kept for a long time in the families' storerooms.

Burial in the ground is reserved for people who died of contagious diseases such as leprosy and smallpox, as well as for robbers, murderers, and other criminals. The law denies them celestial burial and even water burial, for if their souls are trapped underground, they will not be reincarnated and their kind will become extinct. This type of burial, which brings dishonor on the family of the deceased, serves to illustrate how different the Tibetan concept of death and burial is from those current in the West.

Cremation is used for the learned scholar-monks called Geshe, and other highly placed persons. Their bodies are burned, and the bones and ashes are either scattered to the winds or cast into a river.

The most exalted resting place for a person's remains is in one of the Buddhist religious monuments called stupas or chortens. When a lama of exceptional repute dies, his body is washed with salt water and left to dry. It is then rubbed with precious ointments and spices and inurned in the stupa. Only very few are eligible for such inurnment, namely Dalai Lamas, Panchen Lamas, and some other great lamas. Some of the last are cremated, and their ashes are preserved in the stupa. Dalai and Panchen Lamas have stupas plated with gold or silver. Then there are bronze, wooden, and clay stupas, used according to the status of the lama. These stupas are stored in the halls of the monasteries.

The origins of the burial rites in Tibet lie deep in the religious history and legends of the country. It is said that some 2,000 years ago a king called Drigum Tsenpo adopted burial in the tomb; before him there was no such thing, and kings simply rose to the sky. Records of early rites are preserved in *The King's Admonitions* and other Tibetan histories. From the times of King Thothori Nyantsen, who lived around the year 200 of the Christian calendar, it was stipulated that tombs be set up for kings, queens, royal concubines, and princes. The remains of tombs still to be seen in Chunggye in the Yarlung valley are evidence of the early burial of royalty in tombs. When Buddhism became the dominant religion in Tibet, other rites came into use, such as cremation for some great lamas to release their souls in accordance with the Buddhist scriptures.

To Tibetans vultures are sacred birds because of the important part they play in the celestial burial and also because they are believed not to harm any small creatures. They have thus become a protected species, and hunters are not allowed to shoot them. In the water burial, the feeding of a corpse to the fish has the spiritual significance of a gift to the Buddha, and so fulfills the wish to perform good works. In former times fish were considered "gods of the river," and to eat them was contrary to the Buddhist faith.

Marriages in Tibet used to be almost always arranged. Sons and daughters — and especially daughters—had little right to choose their partners and often did not even know what they looked like until the marriage. There was no intermarriage between the rich and the poor, for social position and wealth were the primary factors, with good looks and moral character lagging far behind. Society was divided into eight classes, and people could marry only within their own. For instance, the children of butchers and smiths, who belonged to the lowest class, could not rise out of it by marriage. And intermarriage only within one's own social class naturally tended to perpetuate the rigid class system.

Superstition also played an important role. Before a young man's family made a proposal of marriage, a silk khata had to be presented to the parents of the prospective bride, and at the same time they were asked "the eight characters" and "the shengxiao." The former were arranged in four pairs, and indicated the month, day, and hour of a person's birth; the shengxiao was any one of twelve animals symbolizing the year of birth. These particulars were then taken to a revered lama or fortune teller to see if those of the would-be bride and those of the would-be bridegroom were in mutual agreement. If they were, then the pair could become engaged, and if not, the parents on either side could refuse to consent to the match, however willing the prospective couple might be.

Common serfs could not marry without the approval of their landlords. Generally speaking, it was easier to marry another serf belonging to the same landlord, as marriages between serfs of different landlords meant that one or the other of the landlords lost a serf. It was hard to obtain the permission of the landlords as well as of both sets of parents.

Marriage was also prohibited between relatives. This rule was absolute with regard to the paternal side of the family, while on the mother's side marriage was permitted only after four generations.

Recently more and more young people have been marrying for love, but the old procedures and ceremonies of proposal, engagement, and marriage are still for the most part adhered to. Before a formal proposal is made, a fortune teller must be consulted and a silk khata presented to the family of the young woman. If both parties agree to the marriage, an auspicious day is chosen and a marriage contract is drawn up as a pledge that the couple will love and honor each other, respect their elders, and maintain a high standard of conduct. Sometimes the contract also includes details regarding inheritance. This type of contract is cast in the form of a poem.

After this has been accomplished, the two families join in the following engagement ceremonies: The bridegroom's family present a khata to every member of the bride's family and give the bride's parents "nursing money" as well as a pangden, or apron. The idea behind the apron ritual is that the girl must have worn out a great number of her mother's aprons and this new one is a form of recompense. After the ritual drinking of tea and barley beer, a witness for one side recites the marriage contract, two copies of which are placed on a dish, while a witness for the other side carefully compares the two copies to make sure they tally. Then the witnesses affix the family seals on the contracts, and a representative of each side hands a copy to the father of the other.

On the day before the wedding ceremony the bridegroom sends a fine dress, a headgear called a padru, and bracelets and other ornaments to the bride for her wedding attire. On the day itself the bridegroom sends a mounted representative, accompanied by a retinue, to fetch the bride. With him be brings some colored arrows decorated with mirrors, jade, and pearl ornaments. The bride rides back with the retinue, mounted on a pregnant mare, the color of which must match that of her shengxiao.

But before the arrival of the retinue the bride has to make a symbolic offering of grain from a chyma, or grain dipper, drink some barley beer, and go through a farewell ceremony. On entering the bride's house, the bridegroom's representative attaches the colored arrows to the bride's back as a token that she now belongs to the bridegroom's family, and takes the jade and places it on her head as a sign that the bridegroom's soul is entrusted to her. As the bride leaves, one of her family bearing a colored arrow in one hand and a leg of mutton in the other stands atop the house and shouts, "Don't take away the good luck of our family!" over and over again until she is far away.

At three points along the road there are members of the bridegroom's family waiting to offer refreshments to the procession. If the retinue meets someone carrying water or wood, this is considered lucky and a member of the procession will dismount to present this person with a khata; if the retinue encounters someone carrying an invalid along the road, or someone carrying an empty basket or throwing away rubbish, this is thought of as most inauspicious, and will mean going after the wedding to persuade some lamas to recite Buddhist scriptures to exorcise the bad luck. During the journey to the bridegroom's home all those in the procession sing zhaychen, so-called "great songs," with the exception of the bride, who traditionally sobs.

Before the procession arrives at the bridegroom's house, his family decorate their front door and prepare a mat for the bride to dismount on. This mat is made of bags of highland barley (gingke) and wheat covered with figured satin, on which a Tibetan swastika is traced with grains of wheat sprinkled from a chyma. Members of the family wait at the door, holding the chyma and barley beer.

Tibetan social rituals are many and varied and closely connected with religion. Khatas are presented in an extraordinary variety of situations, in addition to weddings, births, and funerals—for instance, when one calls on one's elders, pays homage to figures of the Buddha, or takes leave of an honored person to make a journey. The khata usually is a piece of raw silk fabric woven almost to the fineness of a spider's web, though it is sometimes made of high-quality satin. Its length varies from 3 feet to as much as 20 feet. The khata is a symbol of purity and sincerity. From time immemorial Tibetans have considered that white symbolizes both purity and good luck, so most khatas are white. But there are also gaily colored khatas in blue, yellow, green, and red, and these are presented to those who have made vows to attain Buddhahood and are wound around the arrows for the bride to give them color. Colored khatas are the grandest gifts of all. According to Buddhist belief, the colored khata is the dress of the Bodhisattva and can therefore be used only on special occasions.

The kowtow—the word comes from Chinese and literally means "to knock the head"—is also an important element of etiquette in Tibet. It is used, for instance, in rendering homage to images of the Buddha and occasionally in paying respects to one's elders. There are three kinds—the long kowtow, the short kowtow, and the "resounding" kowtow. During religious celebrations at the Tsulhakhang Temple the Potala Palace, and other important shrines a visitor will see the crowds kowtow for a long time, raising their hands above their heads, lowering them to their breasts three times, and then prostrating themselves upon the ground. This is the long kowtow.

In the short kowtow, a person kneels and lowers the head and arms to the ground. According to Tibetan records it was formerly a gesture of courtesy used only for the Tsenpos, but later came to be performed before Buddhist monks as well.

The resounding kowtow can be seen only in monasteries, where the kneeling faithful, regardless of age or sex, join their palms in front of their breasts in the attitude of prayer before the statue of the Buddha, bow three times, and then knock their foreheads audibly on the floor. Finally they creep to the foot of the statue and touch the Buddha gently with their heads as a sign of repentance.

On meeting a high official or other important personage, it was customary in the past to take off one's hat and bow to an angle of 45°, holding the hat so low as to almost touch the ground. With less important folk or one's equals a slight bow was enough, with the hat held before the breast. Today people sometimes bow while placing the palms together in an attitude of respect. In greeting important personages, the hands with joined palms should be raised above the head as one bends and nods. This greeting is returned by the other party.

When a guest arrives on a feastday, the Tibetan host must offer barley beer, and the guest has to take one or two small sips before going on to drink the whole cupful. Not to do so would be considered very impolite. Tea drinking is a daily affair, as in many other countries, though the characteristic beverage of Tibet is brick tea churned up with butter. A guest must wait for the mistress of the house or her children to pour out this buttered tea, as it would be very bad manners to do otherwise.

Some of the ritual acts described above are performed every day or many times a day, while others are reserved for particular occasions. All of them, however, are thoroughly characteristic of the Tibetan way of life.

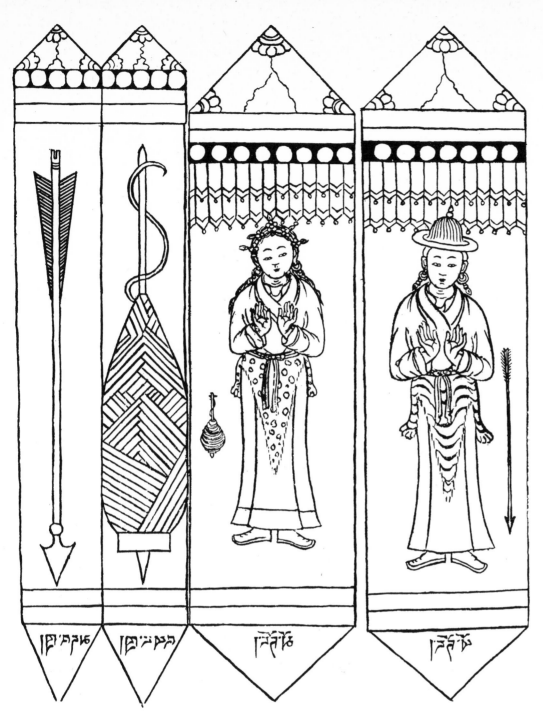

Chapter IV   Women, Marriage, and the Family

Na Zhen

In former times Tibetan women were regarded somewhat as devils in human form. They often were held accountable for misfortunes and disasters. If a woman ploughed the fields, it was said, the ox which she harnessed would die; some believed that seedlings wouldn't grow if they were planted by a woman. In a word, women were seen as people who spelled disaster, the incarnation of bad luck. And in many ways they were hardly treated as human beings at all.

Tibetan women lived under the fourfold oppression of the state, the clan, religion, and the husband. They were powerless in society and subservient in their own families. The old Tibetan legal code included the following stipulations: "Do not let women have the right to discuss affairs of state," and "Women should not be allowed to participate in military and political affairs." A comparatively recent local government code of sixteen articles included one which stated specifically: "Pay no heed to what women have to say," and elsewhere stipulated that if a woman was raped, she should be punished as well as the aggressor because she was naturally "the root of all evil."

These official regulations obviously derive from popular beliefs. There were many Tibetan proverbs and sayings like "Dogs, women, and children are the roots of trouble," or "If you believe what a woman says, the roof of your house will soon be overgrown with weeds," or "A woman's talk is like the galloping of a mare." And the forces of social tradition hedged women about with endless restrictions, established by common practice over the years. For example, women were not allowed to speak loudly or be playful and joke while laboring in the fields; they were not allowed to butcher livestock, or to enter the scripture room of a temple, or to go out of doors without hats and shawls. In some localities the authorities established specific "prohibitory regulations" for women. Should a woman violate any of these regulations and then by coincidence a natural calamity take place, such as a hailstorm or hard frost, some people would unhesitatingly place the blame for it upon that woman.

From ancient times the belief prevailed in Tibet that the male was innately superior to the female, and the humiliating description "kyemei," meaning "low and degrading persons," was applied to women. Understandably, then, when a woman prostrated herself before the Buddha in worship, the first words she said might well be something like "Pray, Buddha, show mercy on me, let me give birth to a son," or "Pray, Buddha, let me be a man in my next life." If a woman did give birth to a son, there would be general satisfaction. Ceremonies to celebrate the incarnation of a male would be held on the third day after the child's birth. But should a girl be born to the family, the ceremonies would be postponed to the fifth day, because it was believed that a girl bore too much hard luck with her and it would not be proper to hold the celebrations too early.

Men and women were treated very differently in matters of upbringing and education. When a boy child was eight years old, his family would do everything possible to have him taught to read and write, and even the poorest family would try their best to get the boy into a lamasery, where he would have the opportunity to study Buddhist scriptures. In the case of girls, most education was considered superfluous. Few women, therefore, were literate.

(Many old women in rural and pastoral areas are even today unaware of the date of their own birth.) Girls of aristocratic and merchant families were hardly exceptions; they were given the barest minimum of teaching, just enough to keep accounts for the family or write a brief letter to a husband when he was away from home.

When boys came of age, at eighteen, they had to learn how to do business and engage in lawsuits, and they were allowed to have a hand in the management of family affairs. When a girl reached fifteen, she had to learn how to milk cows, make barley beer, and wait on the men. Boys and girls were obviously being trained to play widely different roles in society. Another common saying is significant in this respect: "Men can do what they like so long as they don't go mad; women must obey, like tools that have the power of speech."

When a woman married, she was simply adding a servant to her husband's household. In her husband's family a woman had no right of inheritance and no say in the management of the property of the family. In contrast, if a man lived with his wife's family, he might be, and often was, the master of the household, with total control of her family's property.

Under serfdom, serfs were attached absolutely to their landlord owners, and their marriages were arranged first by the owners and then by their parents. If a woman serf wished to marry, her owner's consent had to be acquired beforehand, and if generous gifts were not sent to him, he might very well not give his blessing. If the serf wanted to marry a serf of a different master, money had to be sent to both masters. But the same rules were imposed on the male serfs too. No serfs had freedom in love or marriage. Their masters could award them in marriage as they chose.

Among the common people marriages were then arranged by parents, and their arrangements were sometimes distinctly commercial. For instance, in the pastoral regions of northern Tibet the standard price of a girl was at one time twenty yaks—a payment referred to euphemistically as a "nursing fee." If a girl disagreed with her parents' choice, she might be kidnapped by her future husband. In some such cases her parents would work hand in glove with the man they favored and send their daughter to the village where he lived on the pretext of visiting their relatives or running some errand or other; when the girl arrived, he would abduct her and then make her consent to marry him under duress. This practice is now illegal, though still far from extinct, particularly among the Sherpas.

Remnants of primitive communal marriage systems are also still to be found in Tibet. Most families are now monogamous, but polyandrous and polygamous families and women with temporary spouses are still not rare. According to recent surveys, polygamous families used to account for 5 percent of total families in some regions, and polyandrous families for as many as 24 percent. Polyandrous families are mostly composed of two or three brothers sharing the same wife, and were often formed by the poor in order to lessen certain labor imposed upon them by the landowners, called "wula" labor. In this way the poor could have enough people to supply for wula labor without at the same time holding up their own work in the fields or the pastures. Parents also hoped that a polyandrous arrangement of this kind would encourage the brothers to live together in harmony, and if a wife could make her husbands live together on friendly terms, she was respected and praised by all. In the case of rich families, polandrous marriages also served the practical purpose of preventing the family property from being dispersed among other families.

Polygamous families were mostly to be found among high-ranking officials and noblemen, rather like the landlords and wealthy men in other societies who often maintained several concubines as well as their wives. These aristocrats and bureaucrats adopted polygamy in order to maintain their social status and keep their wealth within the family. If a man's first wife could not or did not bear him a son, then he married another and another and another, until he found one who did; for if there were no male offspring, the household would be left without an heir, and with no one to inherit the social status and property of the family, its wealth would once again be dispersed. Poor families were sometimes polygamous too, but here, as with the polyandrous families but the other way round, several sisters usually shared a common husband. There were also cases of a mother and daughter sharing a husband. This would sometimes happen if the wife's first husband died leaving

a young daughter. The mother would remarry, taking a husband younger than herself in order to support the family, and the daughter, when she came of age, would marry her stepfather.

In rural and pastoral areas many women are unmarried, but they often have with them two or three illegitimate children whom they are responsible for bringing up. This is another indication of the inferior status of women, and one of its main causes has been the prevalence of Lamaism. In former times a large proportion of the male population became lamas and were not allowed to marry. In addition, polyandry was widespread, women were therefore in excess, and one-parent families were the result.

With the recent changes in society, new legislation, and the formation of various women's associations, particularly the Patriotic and Democratic Women's Association of the Tibet Autonomous Region, many of the family and social practices oppressive to women have largely ceased to exist, and women are now found in increasing numbers in the professions, in government, and in sports. A number of distinguished figures have emerged, too, in the fields of scientific research, education, medicine, literature, and art. For girls now have the right to attend school along with the boys. For more than twenty years a considerable number of girls and young Tibetan, Menpa, Lopa, Denpa, and Sherpa women have been getting educations at the Central College for Nationalities, the Southwestern College for Nationalities, and the Northwestern College for Nationalities. In recent years a medical college, a teachers' college, and an agricultural and animal-husbandry college have been established in Tibet, and consequently even more Tibetan girls now have the opportunity of education. Maternity care and child health and hygiene are also given strong emphasis in Tibet today, and a strong population growth rate is one of the results.

Of course much still needs to be done. But as a worker in women's affairs in Tibet I am proud of the progress that has already been made in my country toward the liberation of women.

68. *Even the most recently built houses respect the traditional forms of Tibetan architecture.*

69. *Though Lhasa is an ancient city dating back over 1,300 years, until very recently any substantial building was confined to the monasteries and the palaces of the aristocracy. The common people lived in mud dwellings that were not built to last. In the past twenty years the built-up area of Lhasa has increased ten times, and it is on its way to becoming a modern city.*

71

70. *Such picturesque old buildings as this
are nearly always spruced up with rows of
potted flowers. Comparatively well-off
Tibetans usually live in two-story houses
with the living room on the sunny upper
floor and the kitchen and storerooms below.*

71. *Old Tibetan houses in Palkhor Street
in Lhasa. Cultivating flowers is a hobby
and a matter of pride in Tibetan towns.*

72

73

72. The furniture of Tibetan houses usually includes a pair of painted cupboards, two benches, and a low square table that resembles a chest. Hanging on the wall are New Year pictures and a mirror. Devout Buddhist families keep an altar with an image of the Buddha with water, flowers, and an offering of dried food beneath it.

73. A Tibetan family at mealtime. The highland barley called gingke is the staple food of the Tibetans. Roasted flour made from it is kneaded with butter into the form of cakes and eaten with buttered tea. It is not traditional in Tibet to wear a hat at the table. The boy wanted to show off for the photographer.

74. All over Tibet one sees people churning buttered tea, and a churn such as this is a prime household necessity. The tea is made by boiling brick tea until it is very thick, pouring it into the churn, adding butter and salt, and churning until the tea and butter are perfectly amalgamated.

106

75

76

75. *A street scene in Lhasa.*

76. *Among the wild animals that abound on the Tibetan plateau are leopards, bears, orangutans, wild oxen, wild horses, boars, monkeys, foxes, wolves, deer including musk deer, lynx, and antelope. Musk is an important product, and Tibetan herdsmen make a side occupation of trading in bear's gall and pilose antler. Cooperative stores buy large quantities of furs and valuable medicinal herbs for sale every year.*

77. *Tourists and pilgrims mingle in the streets of Lhasa. Hanging on the line above are a number of lungtas—pieces of cotton that are presented as ceremonial gifts.*

79

80

81

82

78/83. *Tibetan faces.*

84

84. *The market is still very much a part of the Tibetan way of life—the traditional place for both trade and conversation. This is a glimpse of the open-air market at Shigatse.*

85. *Ornaments of all kinds are very popular among the Tibetans. Gold and silver ornaments such as these are made today according to traditional Tibetan techniques, and the craftsmanship is still on the highest level.*

85

86. In Tibet the working of gold and silver
has a history of over a thousand years. The
traditional artifacts include ornaments such
as bracelets, necklaces, and hair ornaments,
elegant knife sheaths and snuff boxes, and
household necessities such as wine cups, tea
bowls, and pots and lids. All remain
uniquely Tibetan in style.

87

88

87. *During the Lingka season—literally "the time of gardens"—old and young come together for picnics in daily decorated tents.*

89

90

88. The Zhotan Festival is an occasion for performances of the Tibetan drama. At one time the troupes of actors had to present their performances before the Dalai Lama at the Norbu Lingka (Jewel Park) but now the performances are open to the public.

89. There are many drinking songs in the Tibetan folksong repertoire, and these old ladies seem to have sung quite a lot of them.

90. The first ten days of July in the Tibetan calendar are the time when everyone bathes in the river, as the river waters are then both clean and warm. Men and women, old and young, can be seen indulging in a pleasure that still retains something of a ritual act of cleansing.

91. People watching a performance of the traditional Tibetan drama during the Zhotan Festival. Song and dance are integral parts of this drama, which dates back at least to the fifteenth century.

117

92

92. *The pride and independence of the people of remotest Tibet are eloquently expressed in the bearing of this nomadic woman. The rifle slung on her back is most unusual. Note the two prongs at the end, which are placed on the ground when firing. This type of rifle is thought to have been invented by the Mongols.*

93. *A young nomad with an amulet around his neck. These hardy and adventurous people may scarcely see the inside of a house as long as they live. This photograph is the last one taken by Yang Minghui, who lost his life in a motor accident during the expedition to take the photographs for this book.*

94. *For safety's sake very young children are tied on horseback during long treks through perilous terrain.*

96

97

95. *The* Four Pharmacopoeias *is an epoch-making work in the history of Tibet. Written 1,100 years ago, it anticipates many of the findings of modern medicine. With regard to the growth of the human embryo, for example, it distinguishes "the fish stage" (corresponding to the aquatic creature), "the tortoise stage" (corresponding to the reptile), and "the pig stage" (corresponding to the mammal).*

96. *A research group has been set up to study historical accounts of Tibet with a view to extending our knowledge of the nation's past.*

97. *Medical instruction in a Tibetan pharmacy.*

98. *Celestial burial is the most common form of burial in Tibet. The undertaker cuts the corpse in small pieces and feeds it to vultures, which are therefore considered to be sacred birds. Only when the whole body has been disposed of is the soul perfectly free to depart from it. This photo shows the burning of pine and cypress wood to attract the vultures.*

99. *Here the undertaker is dissecting the corpse. He pounds the bones, mixes them with tsampa—roasted barley flour—and feeds the mixture to the vultures first. In this way no mortal remains are left, and the soul is set free.*

100. *The final act in the celestial burial, as the sacred vultures dispose of every morsel of the corpse.*

Chapter V   Ethnic Minorities in Tibet

Cai Xiansheng

101. Results of the "cut and burn" process of farming. This primitive form of farming was virtually the only one known to the Lopa people of southeastern Tibet until twenty years ago.

The Tibetan plateau covers 460,000 square miles and has a population of about 1,650,000 people. Ethnic Tibetans make up 96 percent of this population, but there are more than ten racial minorities. We will here describe some of the most important and interesting of these minority groups.

The largest of the minority groups of Tibet is the Menpas, who number 40,000. They are mostly concentrated in southern and eastern areas such as Meito, Tshona, and Nyingkhri. Among the smaller groups, the Lopas straddle a long stretch of the southern frontier in southeastern Tibet, and the Denpas are scattered throughout the southeastern region of Chayu. There are Sherpas grouped in Dram on the Nepalese border and the Chentang and Rongxia areas. Sherpas also live in the kingdom of Nepal, where they are called "She'erpas." In the Tibetan language "Sherpa" means "easterner," and the Sherpas claim to have immigrated long ago from Sichuan and other areas. The Nakhi, or Naxis, live in the Chiangjiang (Yangtze) Valley and toward the Burmese border.

In former times the minority peoples of Tibet were often disparaged and treated badly. For instance, in ancient Tibetan the very word "Lopa" meant "savage" (now the meaning has changed and it means "southerner").
But the geographic isolation of the Menpas, Lopas, Denpas, and Sherpas is the reason why a hard and primitive way of life persisted among them for so long. What agriculture they had was based on the "cut and burn" principle. This process prevents many plants which would otherwise grow from getting a hold and limits the flora to a few fireproof species. The attitude of these peoples toward this kind of farming is summed up in these lines:

Set fire to the wilderness,
Dig holes with sticks,
Sow a handful of seeds,
And leave the rest to fate.
Harvests are the gifts of heaven,
Failures the will of Providence.

With such methods of agriculture, they lived mainly by hunting and gathering wild berries and roots.

Their very way of life determined the method by which products were distributed among the members of the community. The Lopas still preserve a system dating from very ancient and primitive times. They go hunting in groups and distribute the game equally among the members of the community, except that by tradition the animal hides and heads go to the hunter who scored the first hit. The family with the greatest number of such trophies enjoys the most prestige. A similar method of distribution was used, and to a certain extent is still used, among the Menpas, Denpas, and Sherpas.

Most of these people lived in huts built of branches and banana leaves, and their clothing was made entirely of leaves and wild hemp. Some lived in houses built of wood placed on piles and capped by flat stones, houses whose only entrance was through a trap door in the floor. The axe was the main and virtually the only building implement known to these peoples. They used it to fell trees, trim logs, split boards, smooth out surfaces, and so on. With the axe they made thin boards for their roofs, stouter ones for their floors and walls, and timbers for uprights and beams. On the other hand, these peoples lived surrounded by virgin forests, so they had plenty of wood to use as their main building material, instead of building the mud and stone structures characteristic of the rest of Tibet. And their way of life with all its privations largely prevented the development of their sense of private ownership, so when a new house was being built, the entire tribe would turn out and lend a hand for nothing and this remains their custom.

Such customs are important compensations, but it remains true that the age-old way of life of these ethnic minorities doomed them to bare subsistence, and that this way of life still exists among them to a large extent. Since reforms introduced in 1959, however, these peoples have been introduced to new methods of production and are becoming a part of the Tibetan nation.

Another sign of change among them has to do with language. The Menpas, Denpas, and Sherpas have their own languages but never acquired written language, and without it these peoples remained in a state in which they kept count of the days by tying knots and recorded events by notching sticks. The whole idea of keeping track of days and years was foreign to these peoples, and until recently almost no one knew his own age. But now they are increasingly coming to use Tibetan.

The Menpas, Lopas, Denpas, and Sherpas each have their own ideas about food. A staple food of the Menpas consists of buckwheat pancakes cooked on a thin stone slab and washed down with thick pepper soup. The Lopas also like buckwheat pancakes, but as hunters they tend to add roast meats, dried meat, and milk curd to their diet. Corn and "chicken-claw rice," a kind of millet, are staple foods for the Denpas, who incidentally are also confirmed smokers and drinkers. A common dish for the Sherpas is a thick corn porridge, called gongze, and steamed potatoes.

As with many peoples living in primitive conditions, hospitality is of the greatest importance to these peoples. The moment you cross the threshold of a Denpa house, you will be offered a bowl of white home-brewed wine. If you are a guest in a Lopa house, it is a breach of good manners to leave a dish unfinished. Here it is still the custom for the host to taste the food on the table as a token of sincerity, to show that it is not poisoned, before a guest is asked to partake of it. Needless to say, in these days the gesture is purely symbolic.

The easiest way of distinguishing these four peoples from one another is by their clothes. The Menpa men and women of Lepo wear robes of deep red phulu, a kind of thick woolen cloth, with trident-shaped caps of the same color hemmed around with orange. Menpa women wear white aprons and on special occasions put on bracelets, necklaces, and earrings. Everyone both old and young wears a piece of calf hide on his back and a pair of Tibetan embroidered knee boots. The Menpas of Meito dress more or less like the Tibetans, though the Menpa women may be distinguished by their gaily colored striped skirts.

Lopa men wear short pullover waistcoats and always carry with them a saber and bow and arrows as symbols of masculinity. The standard wear for Lopa women is a round-necked, narrow-sleeved blouse and a tartan-like barrel-shaped skirt that comes down over the knees. Another way of telling

Lopas and Menpas apart is that the former, both men and women, wear their hair long. In front it is cut in a fringe coming right down to their brows, while the rest of their hair flows down onto their shoulders. Both sexes love ornaments of every kind. The men wear bamboo necklaces and earrings. A Lopa woman in her full panoply, dressed up for some festive occasion, is often seen with a dozen or more strings of beads, not to mention bracelets, earrings, silver coins, bronze bells, iron chains, knives, and shells. The whole outfit may weigh as much as 15 pounds.

Living in the subtropical zone called the Jiangnan to the south of the Changjiang River, famous as Tibet's "land of plenty," the Denpa men wear sleeveless gowns and shorts, while the women have short-sleeved blouses just long enough to cover the bosom, with long skirts to match. Both men and women wear shawls and carry haversacks of a characteristic design. All Denpa men and women are addicted smokers. The first thing one notices on entering a Denpa village is likely to be that everyone carries a long pipe with a tobacco pouch dangling from it. In the pouch are dried tobacco leaves, which are crunched in the hand and dropped into the pipe. The men also carry a few chips of resinous wood so that with a flint and a little dry grass for tinder they can start a fire whenever they like. They secure this resinous wood by selecting a big tree and burning it on one side, which seems to attract the resin to the burned spot. The charred bark is sliced away, and pieces of wood are cut from the trunk. The men wear bamboo hats to keep off the rain. The women put up their hair in buns at the back of their necks and wear large silver ornaments on their foreheads, earrings the size of a hand plus funnel-shaped ornaments in their earlobes, and strings of pearls around their necks. All these regalia make Denpa women unmistakable.

The Sherpas are addicted to cleanliness, and their standard wear is a white phulu jacket which opens down the front and is also called a "baiduo." The women wear "gelong" trousers flaring at the hem and a kind of skirt that fastens at the front. The men wear shorts, with a kind of white waistband called a gase and a belt called a gabu. Tucked into the belt as a mark of masculinity is a hunting knife.

The Menpas and the Sherpas are both Lamaists, Tibetan Buddhists, in religion. The Dawang Temple is one of their chief shrines. The Sixth Dalai Lama, the celebrated poet Tsangyang Gyatso, was of Menpa extraction. The Lamaist temples of the Sherpas are in Dram and Chengtang. The older Sherpas have altars in their rooms stacked with the Buddhist scriptures, and before these altars they worship and pay homage to the Buddha.

The Lopas and the Denpas both are professed nature fetishists, and the Lopas practice divination and exorcism. On occasions such as marriages, funerals, the laying of foundations, sowing crops, or starting on journeys, the Lopas kill chickens to see if the grain of the liver is propitious for the undertaking. An average Lopa family will kill about seventy or eighty chickens a year for such purposes. Sometimes a day's killing may amount to ten or twenty, as they go on until a propitious liver is found.

On the whole the Menpas, Denpas, and Sherpas practice monogamy. The commercial aspect of marriage was important in the past and to a certain extent still is. To gain a Menpa bride, the prospective bridegroom has on three separate occasions to make gifts of wine, meat, money, and valuables. Sometimes the "price" is as high as three or four head of dzo, or even as many as a dozen. Until recent times Denpa women were openly bought with buffaloes, pigs, chicken, or meat, and a married woman is not in the least shy about telling the price that was paid for her. Denpa men can sell their wives without the least stain attaching to them in the community. The moment she steps into his house, a Denpa woman becomes part of her husband's property, and if her husband dies, she if rightfully inherited by his brother or some other close relative bearing the same surname.

So among the Sherpas abduction-marriages are still an accepted custom. If a girl wants to marry the young man she loves, she may have to contrive to get herself abducted by him. This form of marriage can be expedient when the girl and her parents do not see eye to eye about the matter. And there are cases when the parents conspire with their would-be son-in-law to abduct their stubborn daughter. But things do not end with a successful abduction, and the match must be sanctioned with a marriage ceremony at which the guests drink and dance and make merry until dawn.

The Tibetans usually practice celestial burial for their dead. The Menpas, Denpas, and Sherpas,—with the exception of the Lepo Menpas, whose funeral practices are similar to those of the Tibetans—almost never practice celestial burial. Cremation is quite common among both Denpas and Sherpas. The dead body of a Sherpa is placed in a wooden coffin and burned on a pyre of wood. Some of the ashes are later scattered over the waters of a river. But for Sherpa infants a kind of celestial burial is the invariable rule. The child's body is exposed in a mountain cave to be devoured by birds of prey and other wild animals. The Denpa cremation ceremony is a good deal more sophisticated. The body lies in state in a special shed from one to three days, and relatives lament over it day and night. Then guns are fired and firecrackers set off to awaken the dead person's soul before the body is finally cremated. Burial in the ground, which the Tibetans reserve for criminals and people with contagious diseases, is the standard practice of the Lopas. The dead person is dressed in new clothes, arranged in a sitting posture, covered with a clean sheet, bound with a piece of rope, and placed behind a door. Two or three days later the corpse is carried to the burial ground. There the rope is slackened, and the body is straightened out and lowered into a pit about 10 feet deep. It is covered first with boards and then with clay.

The Nakhi believe that a silver coin must be placed on the tongues of dying people so that they will gain immediate entrance into paradise. Family members who are ill or very old are watched constantly so that the moment of passing will not go unobserved. It is considered a great calamity to die suddenly. The soul of the unfortunate person who does is condemned to perpetual wandering until special ceremonies are performed to release it. Among the Nakhi another traditional belief is that the dead can be consulted in time of crisis such as severe illness. A professional medium is summoned, and chants incantations, dances a little, and then falls into a trance. The dead relay their prophecies or prescriptions to the family through the medium, and all instructions are faithfully followed and regarded as infallible.

102. A Menpa community in a mountain village. There are about 40,000 Menpas in Tibet, mostly concentrated in southern and eastern areas.

103. A team of packhorses on their way to market with a consignment of churns for making buttered tea. Modern roads and transport facilities are still scarce in remote areas.

104

105

104. *Menpa girls on their way to school. Menpa villages now have their own schools and teachers.*

105. *Wooden aqueducts of this kind bring water to Menpa homes in the mountains.*

106. *"Lao zhu ba" is the Menpa name for a skilled maker of wooden bowls. The bowls are essential household equipment for the Menpas, as well as for the Lopas and the Tibetans themselves.*

107. *The Menpas, who live in remote and densely forested mountain areas still use the bow and arrow to hunt birds and wild animals.*

109

110

108. A Lopa hunter and his dog. The Lopas usually hunt in groups, and their bag is distributed throughout the community. The whole village turns out to welcome the men back home. If a tiger is bagged, the hunter who scored the first hit is feted and presented with a tiger-skin cap as a trophy.

109. The women of the minority peoples wear ornaments that distinguish them from the other peoples. This woman is a Lopa.

110. A group of pretty Lopa girls.

111. The Lopa men of the Leyu area are hunters who still live very close to nature. Here a Lopa man at work with his all-purpose knife still has his bow slung on his back. He and his wife share their modest fire with a dog and a bear cub.

113

114

*112. A Sherpa couple. More and more
Sherpas now choose their marriage
partners of their own free will, though
abduction-marriages still occasionally take
place as they used to.*

*113. Lopa houses are usually built on
slopes so as to get as much sunlight as they
possibly can.*

*114. A Nepalese nun of Sherpa origin on a
visit to relatives on the Tibetan side of the
border.*

*115. Sherpa men and women in their
phulu jackets, which in their language they
call "baiduo."*

116

116. *All Denpas are ferocious smokers, including the women, and are usually seen with their pipes in their mouths. This woman is wearing her full regalia of finely worked silver ornaments, including the characteristic Denpa earrings.*

117. *Barefoot Denpa men wearing turbans. Living as they do in one of the mildest climates in Tibet, they wear fairly scanty clothing.*

118. *Three generations of a Denpa family.*

119

Chapter VI Tibetan Buddhism

Jampei Chinlei
edited by Fosco Maraini

119. *Padmasambhava, or Padma Jungnai in Tibetan, was a native of Udyana in present-day Pakistan and a great master of occult Buddhism. He was invited to Tibet to teach King Trisong Detsen during the eighth century, and greatly inspired the Nyingma-pa sect, sometimes called "the Old Sect," of Tibetan Buddhism, or Lamaism.*

During the early centuries of the Christian calendar the scattered tribes occupying the Tibetan uplands became united under a dynasty of kings with their ancestral home in the region of Yarlung, south of the Yarlung Tsangpo River and southeast of Lhasa. The unification of the country, its internal stability, and, soon, a series of military conquests extending the sway of the kingdom over larger and larger territories brought about previously unknown prosperity and a measure of social advancement, at least among the ruling elite. Conquests extended contacts with neighboring countries, such as north India under the Gupta empire and later under its successor states, Nepal, and western China, then ruled by the emperors of the Tang dynasty (618–907).

The Tibetan kingdom, very naturally, came into contact with Buddhism, one of the major world religions in the heyday of its vigor and expansion. Buddhism had originated about a thousand years earlier, in the borderland between India and Nepal, from the preaching of the ascetic Gautama, of princely birth, known to his followers as the Buddha, "the Enlightened One," who came to be called also Sakyamuni, "belonging to the Sakya clan" (probable dates 563–480 B.C.). His teaching is essentially contained in the so-called "four noble truths": that misery is an inevitable part of life; that misery originates from desire; that desire can be eliminated; and that the overcoming of desire, and hence suffering, is made possible by following the eightfold path of virtue:

1. Right understanding (free from superstition and delusion).
2. Right thought (high and worthy of the human intelligence).
3. Right speech (kindly and truthful).
4. Right actions (peaceful, honest, and pure).
5. Right livelihood (bringing hurt or danger to no living being).
6. Right effort (in self-training and self-control).
7. Right mindfulness (having an active, watchful mind).
8. Right concentration (in deep meditation on the realities of life).

Spiritual progress takes place over a succession of reincarnations, the nature of which is governed by the law of karma—deeds good or bad and their consequences. Morality (right action), contributing to the extinction of karma, prohibits the taking of life, human or animal, forbids stealing and lying, enjoins chastity, and fosters brotherly love.

These simple, though demanding, principles soon became intimately interwoven with the immensely complex fabric of Indian thought, and both an elaborate philosophical system and a great world religion took shape.

Though a number of general councils were held by the growing brotherhood of the Buddhist faithful, by around the middle of the third century B.C. the community had become divided into various groups. Two of these were, and have since remained, fundamental: on the one hand there is Hinayana—"the Lesser Vehicle," called by its followers Therevada, "the Way of the Ancients"—more conservative, possibly nearer to the original teachings of the founder, which spread over much of south and southeast Asia; on the other hand there is Mahayana Buddhism, "the Greater Vehicle," which spread over northern India, Kashmir, central Asia, China, Korea, Japan—and Tibet.

The differences that separate the two versions of the Buddhist faith are many and important. Briefly stated, in Therevada schools the historical Buddha retains his central position; the psychology of salvation is definitely more important than any metaphysical problem; and a person seeking salvation aims at reaching the state of an Arhat, "a Worthy One," who has attained the blissful serenity called nirvana through the extinction of karma. The Mahayana schools, on the other hand, see the historical Buddha as an earthly incarnation of an eternal, cosmic Buddha; there is both a rich development of metaphysical thought and a prodigious proliferation of celestial persons (eternal Buddhas and their emanations, deities, major and minor, protectors of the faith, saints and their disciples, angels, mythical beings); and the Arhat ideal gives way to the Bodhisattva ideal. An Arhat, "a Worthy One," has attained salvation and accepts his individual beatitude; a Bodhisattva, on the contrary, attains illumination but postpones the enjoyment of celestial bliss, remaining actively present in the cycle of births and deaths until every sentient being shall have reached complete deliverance from suffering. As one immediately realizes, the Bodhisattva ideal contains a highly inspiring message of love, charity, and altruism, a message which has never failed to enamor the Mahayana faithful and has guaranteed the spreading of their message over such a large proportion of Asia.

Simplified Scheme of Late Mahayana Buddhist Conception of Universal History.

Ages, or kalpas, of the world		
1 2 3	4	5
Past kalpas	The present kalpa	Future kalpa
Presiding celestial Buddha	Avalokitesvara (in Tibetan, Chenresi)	
Presiding celestial Bodhisattva	Amitabha, "Boundless Light" (in Tibetan, Opame)	
Human incarnation	Gautama, the historical Buddha (563–480 B.C.)	Maitreya (in Tibetan, Champa)

The Dalai Lama is conceived, by the faithful, as being a living incarnation of the Bodhisattva Chenresi; the abbot of the Trashilungapo Monastery, the Panchen Lama, is thought to incarnate Opame.

Manjushri, a youthful Bodhisattva whose worship confers retentive memory and intellectual perfection.

Mahayana Buddhism, in a later but significant stage, also posits the existence of five great cosmic ages (kalpa) spread over aeons of time, the present being the fourth. Each age is presided over by a celestial Buddha, by a celestial Bodhisattva, and by his human incarnation. Our kalpa evolves under the supreme Buddha Amitabha and under the Bodhisattva Avalokitesvara, "He Who Looks Down" with pity at suffering; the earthly incarnation of this divine person is the ascetic Gautama, who announced the faith some 2,500 years ago. This spectacular metaphysical construction is complex, and possibly bewildering, but it should be kept in mind for a complete understanding of Tibetan religion. (See Simplified Scheme of Late Mahayana Buddhist Conception of Universal History.)

There is a legend that during the reign of Thothori Nyantsen, a protohistorical king preceding by five generations the great Songtsen Gampo, a sacred Buddhist scripture, a repository for relics (a stupa, or in Tibetan, chorten), and other unspecified religious objects fell to earth near the primitive prehistoric palace called the Yumbu Lagang, which still stands in southern Tibet. Tibetans, however, had no knowledge of writing at that period, no one could understand the meaning of the scriptures, and the strange treasures were simply put away into safekeeping. It was only five kingly generations later that the meaning of these mysterious messages was understood.

According to more credible traditions Buddhism came to Tibet around 630, under King Songtsen Gampo. Some historical records say the king was converted to the new faith by his two consorts, Princess Bhrikuti Devi of Nepal and Princess Wen Cheng of China. Tradition has it also that the main and most sacred Buddhist image called the Jowo, in the Tsulhakhang Temple, or Jokhang, at Lhasa, representing the Buddha Gautama not in his usual monkish garb but as a crowned Bodhisattva, is the one brought to Tibet by the Chinese princess.

It is most probable that Buddhism initially appealed to the Tibetans as a superior form of magic and healing art. Buddhism must have also immensely impressed the comparatively barbaric Tibetans for the marvelously rich and refined civilization accompanying the religious message—for its architecture, sculpture, painting, for its music and liturgy, for its writing and illuminated texts, for its religious garments, its decorative arts, its use of perfumes, lighting, artistic arrangements of offerings, and so on. Becoming a Buddhist, at a certain moment in history, meant graduating from primitive uncouthness to a superior stage in civilization.

Buddhism also compelled people to learn how to read, so as to understand the sacred scriptures, and to write so as to copy them. With Buddhism, Korea and Japan adopted the ideographic script of the Chinese; the Tibetans looked south, to India, for inspiration. A young and brilliant scholar, Thonmi Sambhota, adapted the Indian Gupta script, with a number of ingenious changes, to the Tibetan language of his time. Thus Tibetan script, though complicated because it has retained the archaic spelling, has a pleasing elegance and graphic rhythm all its own.

The religion prevailing in Tibet before the introduction of Buddhism is generally referred to as Bon. Buddhism did not completely supplant Bon, but as happened in Japan with Shinto, it came to a compromise lasting through the centuries up to our days. The entire subject of ancient Bon (which possibly was known under a completely different name, Tsu) is now undergoing intensive revision because of new and more accurate readings of some extremely interesting documents discovered in the caves of Tun Huang, going back to the seventh and eighth centuries of the Christian calendar. Tun Huang is a small town situated where the Silk Road started off from China on its adventurous course across central Asia, and for some decades was in Tibetan hands during the ninth century.

It would be premature to give here a complete picture of primitive Bon, though it appears certain that the Tibetan kings were objects of a divine cult and were considered manifestations of sky gods. Oracular priests called Bon-po had great importance, and blood sacrifice, generally animal but sometimes human, was offered to the gods of the sky, the earth, and the nether world. Many of the deities appear to have been, more often than not, inimical to man, and were imagined as having terrifying aspects. A number of these ferocious gods were later absorbed into Buddhism as "protectors of the faith," and can be seen to this day, painted or sculpted in all their horrid splendor, in objects of Tibetan art.

The traditional account of the Bon religion and its development, now questioned in most of its details, and obviously in its more legendary traits, goes as follows:

Before the introduction of Buddhism the religion of the Tibetans was a primitive form of shamanism called Bon. The story goes that during the reign of the sixth Tsenpo (king) of the ancient Yarlung dynasty a thirteen-year-old boy called Shen was carried away by demons from Ü-Tsang. Ü is the region around Lhasa, Tsang the region in which Gyantse and Shigatse stand, so in terms of civilization Ü-Tsang makes up the very heart of Tibet, though it is in the south geographically. When he came home thirteen years later, now aged twenty-six, he was endowed with such extraordinary powers of prophecy, as well as the ability to subdue demons, that he was named Shenrab, "the Supreme Teacher," and proclaimed a god. Shenrab used no scriptures and preached no doctrine; he taught only how to pray for blessings and keep evil spirits away. In Tibetan religious history this period is known as Dur Bon, or "primitive" Bon.

It is said that when the seventh Tsenpo, Drigun Tsenpo, was murdered by a rival, his descendants called in Bon-po, Bon priests, from the west of Tibet and Kashmir with a view to taking their revenge, and they brought a new wave of Bon. The Bon-po pandit Shamta Ngunpo then incorporated the theories of six heretics, Buddha's contemporaries, with the concepts of indigenous Bon. The result of this is what we call Char Bon.

In the latter half of the eighth century Buddhism began to flourish under the patronage of King Trisong Detsen. However, another Bon scholar retaliated by manipulating the Buddhist canon into faked Bon scriptures. This so infuriated the king, or Tsenpo that he had this scholar executed and commanded all followers of Bon to adopt Buddhism instead. But in the tenth century other Bon-po continued to pillage the Buddhist scriptures to enrich those of Bon, and the historians refer to this phase as Gyur Bon.

A Buddhist mystic monogram. From the seven-
petal lotus an auspicious monogram emerges.
Above are the crescent moon and the sun. The
entire structure is enclosed by a protecting halo.

As a result of the king's order for the compulsory conversion of Bon followers to Buddhism, the old religion began to split into three main schools, namely the White Bon, which is closely akin to Buddhism; the Black Bon, which retains all its original characteristics and is quite different from Buddhism; and the Tra Bon, which is a mixture of the two religions.

Around 775 King Trisong Detsen invited the famous Buddhist teachers Padmasambhava and Santarakshita to come up to Tibet from Kashmir and from India to preach the Buddhist Law among his subjects. It was under the guidance of these two illustrious pandits that the first Buddhist monastery, Samye, was built in Tibet, around 779. On this occasion the first Tibetan monks were ordained and the translation of the Buddhist canon was undertaken in earnest. Shortly thereafter the king gathered together a number of eminent Indian and Chinese masters of Buddhism; this important meeting is known to history as the Council of Lhasa. By lucky chance a detailed report of the council was found among the documents of Tun Huang, and has been published and translated into French by the famous sinologist Paul Demiéville (see Bibliography). The Chinese masters represented the Chan school of thought (in Japanese, Zen) and stood for sudden illumination, for what might be called "instant salvation"; the Indians, led by the pandit Kamasila, were "gradualists," standing for salvation as a long and progressive spiritual ascent. The Indians won the day. This crucial event established the nature and development of Tibetan Buddhism up to our own times.

Under King Thitsu Detsen, better known as Ralpachen, who reigned from 815 to 838, new translations of Buddhist texts and revisions of the older ones were undertaken on a large scale by Tibetan and Indian scholars working in collaboration. As Buddhism spread among the Tibetans under royal sponsorship, religion, as a living institution, became part of the social organization, and many practical problems of integrating it had to be solved. It is known, for instance, that during this period every fully ordained Buddhist priest was allotted seven households to be responsible for his maintenance. This particular form of taxation was the basis from which developed much of the later economic power of Tibetan monasteries, some of them very large, numbering hundreds or even thousands of monks.

Under King Ralpachen Buddhism was fervently supported by the court, possibly antagonizing many of the noble families who retained their faith in the ancient indigenous religion. The Buddhist Ushangdo Chapel had now been built on the east bank of the Lhasa River, and here, it is said, the king would sit with his hair parted and plaited, surrounded with silks and brocades, offering splendid hospitality to Buddhist monks — a gesture of great respect toward the religion. In such a climate Buddhism prospered and flourished as never before. Thus was climaxed the period of over 200 years between Kings Songtsen Gampo and Ralpachen which is known to Tibetan historians as "the Earlier, or First, Spread of Buddhism."

Ralpachen's zeal in promoting the Buddhist faith brought him to disaster: a conspiracy was formed among anti-Buddhist opponents and the king was murdered. His successor, a brother called Lang Darma, who reigned from 838 to 842, was more amenable to the anti-Buddhist, pro-Bon point of view, and the foreign religion was fiercely persecuted. Some Buddhist monks, however, resisted the king; one of them, Lhalung Palgye Dorje by name, managed to conceal a bow and arrow among his vestments and shot the apostate sovereign to death. The fearful crisis which ensued practically set an end to the great Tibetan kingdom, which had held sway over higher Asia for over two centuries. In the heyday of its glory, under Trisong Detsen in the second half of the eighth century, it included, apart from Tibet proper, most of the lands which are now in the Chinese provinces of Qinghai, Gansu, and Yunnan and considerable portions of Sichuan; in the west it extended to Baltistan and Gilgit at the foot of the Karakoram Mountains; in the north it included the Tarim basin with its oases, the Tsaidam marshes, and the neighboring regions, with the famous town of Tun Huang; in the south it claimed Nepal and important portions of India. During the year 763 the Tibetans even marched on the Chinese capital, which they occupied for a few days.

After 842 this vast empire collapsed. For over 150 years Tibet reverted to barbarism, disorder, and ignorance; religious, cultural, and literary activities were reduced to nil. Some surviving members of the royal family managed to found small successor kingdoms in outlying regions of Tibet, especially in the west—for instance, in Ladakh in the upper Indus valley and at Guge in the upper Satlej valley. A few Buddhist monks escaped to Kham, in eastern Tibet, under the guidance of the famous teacher Gongpa Rabsal, "the All-wise" (about 832–915). But the flame of Buddhism was all but extinguished by the followers of the Bon religion, such as Zhigo Lugar, who freely translated and adapted Buddhist scriptures to his own faith. Buddhism was misinterpreted and seriously undermined.

Signs of a Buddhist renaissance appeared in the late tenth century in western Tibet, due in great part to the efforts of a king of Guge who became a monk, taking the name Yeshe-Ö, "Light of Knowledge". Yeshe-Ö feared that what little survived of Buddhism was far from consonant with orthodox teachings, and he therefore sent a number of young subjects to study in India. One of these, Rinchen Zangpo (958–1055), became a famous translator of sacred texts into Tibetan and founded a number of temples and monasteries. Yeshe-Ö was also instrumental in inviting to Tibet the great Indian pandit Atisha (982–1055), who after a number of refusals finally arrived, in 1042, and instructed a large number of disciples at various places until his death twelve years later.

Atisha's teachings aimed at bringing about, among his pupils, a harmonious combination of monastic discipline, ritual practice, and intellectual development. He believed that the Bodhisattva ideal should be realized through gradual stages of spiritual progress aided by strict morality, study, and meditation. He was firm on abolishing the baser, more orgiastic forms of Buddhist initiation and worship which had become popular in Tibet, especially among those who had been influenced by Padmasambhava and his school.

Atisha's foremost disciple, Gyalwai Chungne, better known as Drom Tonpa (1004–1064), founded the now famous monastery of Reting (in Tibetan, Rva Sgreng) north of Lhasa. By this time Buddhism, which had suffered such severe setbacks from the persecutions of Lang Darma, was fully revived. The period of this Buddhist renaissance is known to Tibetans as "the

Later, or Second, Spread of Buddhism," and also as "the rising of Buddhism from the embers."

After the eleventh century Buddhism flourished luxuriantly. Tibet, having lost its political unity and military power, was fragmented into a number of small, practically independent territories continuously fighting each other, and this in itself favored the growth of religious influence among the people; it also encouraged ambitious lamas to enter the fray as heads of ever more powerful monastic institutions. It was during this period that Tibetan Buddhism became diversified into a number of sects. The following principal ones, among many, must be mentioned here.

The Nyingma-pa are the only sect surviving from the Earlier Spread of Buddhism ending in the ninth century, especially from the missionary activities of Padmasambhava (in Tibetan, Guru Rimpoche, "the Precious Master"). The very name of the sect means "Those of the Ancient Teachings." In many parts of Tibet and China the followers of this sect, who wear red hoods and garments, are known as "Red Caps." Padmasambhava, more than a saintly recluse or a learned theologian, is said to have been a most powerful exorcist, magician, and wonder-worker, perfectly versed in all aspects of Tantric Buddhism. The Nyingma-pa are primarily Tantric Buddhists. "Tantra" (in Tibetan, Gyud) is an Indian word originally meaning "thread" or "cord," a word symbolizing the succession of masters and disciples, linked one to the other by initiations to secret doctrines and rites passed from mouth to ear. Later the word was used when speaking of the books in which part of such teachings were consigned to a written form. Tantra schools rely heavily on the recitation of sacred, often secret formulas (mantras), on the use of symbols, such as ritual gestures (mudras), and on cosmic diagrams (mandalas), as means of reaching a subtle identification with superhuman powers.

One of the most characteristic liturgical objects of Tantric masters is the so-called "vajra" (in Tibetan, dorje), a short wand variously wrought, generally of metal, representing a thunderbolt but also symbolizing a perfect and indestructible diamond and in some contexts functioning as a phallic metaphor. The entire complex of Tantric teachings and practices came to be

known, around the sixth century, as Vajrayana, "the Vajra Vehicle," a third and final stage in the development of Buddhism following and completing, according to its believers, both ancient Hinayana and later Mahayana. More debased forms of Vajrayana leaned heavily on magical beliefs and practices, and on its bipolar symbolism, in which male-female oppositions were very important and often developed into liturgies of a highly sexual and sometimes erotic character.

In its earlier stages, the followers of Nyingma-pa relied solely on oral teaching of their doctrines, implying that a true mystical transmission of knowledge, often of a secret nature, can take place only when uttered from master's mouth to pupil's ear. It was in the eleventh century that the first Nyingma-pa monasteries came into existence. By then a number of "hidden scriptures" (in Tibetan, terma), authored according to legend by Padmasambhava himself, had been "discovered" and the sect possessed a large theological summa. Essential Nyingma-pa doctrines stress the unsubstantiality of the phenomenal world and the possibility, for those who have reached certain exalted stages of secret wisdom, of obtaining sudden enlightenment and Buddhahood.

The Sakya sect takes its name from its chief monastery, which rises at Sakya ("tawny soil") in the district of Tsang, south of the Yarlung Tsangpo River. The walls of Sakya monasteries are easily identified because of their wide vertical painted stripes of red, white, and black, symbolizing the three great Bodhisattvas Jampeyang (in Sanskrit, Manjusri), Chenresi (in Sanskrit, Avalokitesvara), and Chanadorje (in Sanskrit, Vajrapani). Because of these colors Sakya monks are commonly known in China as belonging to "the Multicolored Sect." The Sakya sect was founded in the eleventh century by Khon Konchog Gyalpo, a member of the ancient Khon family. He learned the older Tantric Buddhism from his father, then traveled a great distance to learn new forms of Tantrism from Dromi Lotsawa, "Dromi the Translator" (992–1072). In 1073 Khon Konchog Gyalpo founded the first monastery of the Sakya sect near the river Trom, a tributary of the Yarlung Tsangpo.

Khon Konchog Gyalpo decided from the very start that succession of the abbots of the monastery—and later, as it happened, of the entire sect—should be limited to the members of the Khon family, who, moreover, were to keep political and religious powers tightly united in their hands. The earliest five abbots of the monastery, beginning with Khon Konchog Gyalpo, are known as "the five pontiffs of Sakya." The fourth and fifth of the line—Kunga Gyaltsen (1182–1251), called Sakya Pandita ("the Sakya Teacher"), and his famous nephew Phagpa Lodro Gyaltsen (1235–1280)—came suddenly to the fore in Tibetan politics when they were summoned to Liangzhou, the capital of Gansu province in northwestern China, by Godan, a grandson of the immensely powerful Mongol conqueror Genghis Khan. Here an agreement was reached for the submission of Ü and Tsang to the rule of the Mongols. Owing to the diplomatic ability and the prestige of the high Sakya lamas, or religious lords, as they are sometimes called, Mongol rule over Tibet took the form of a near-nominal suzerainty. Sakya Pandita addressed a famous open letter to all Tibetans urging them to abide peacefully by the agreements reached with the Mongol prince: "If we Tibetans help the Mongols in matters of religion, they in turn will support us in temporal matters" (Bibliography, "History and General," Shakabpa, p. 63).

On the Pandita's death in 1251, his place was taken by his nephew Phagpa. This brilliant young cleric is credited with having given a Buddhist initiation of the Tantric school to Kublai Khan, the new Mongol sovereign. When Kublai Khan, after a victorious campaign, became emperor of China in 1260, he proclaimed Phagpa his Tishri (in Chinese, Tishih), that is, "Imperial Preceptor." In the first year of the new Yuan dynasty that Kublai Khan founded, a central board for the "spreading of governance" was set up to control Buddhist affairs in all territories under Mongol rule, and Phagpa received an investiture from Kublai granting him supreme authority over Tibet. A few years later, in 1269, Kublai conferred the title of "Great Precious Lord of the Law" on Phagpa, in recognition of his services and also his invention of a new Mongolian script.

The teachings of the Sakya sect are on the whole eclectic, not substantially different from those of the Kagyu-pa sect, discussed below; what renders the Sakya sect unique, at least in this early period of Tibetan history, is the attention it paid to church organization and its worldly commitment. The early Sakya pontiffs combined in their persons the splendor of temporal princes and lofty spiritual authority. Later on, however, much of the spiritual charisma was lost.

The Kagyu-pa take their name from the word "Kagyu," meaning "oral transmission of the doctrine from master to disciple." This is an important point in most Tibetan Buddhist sects; the exalted position of the master (lama) in the moral, intellectual, and spiritual progress of his disciples is shown by the very fact that the entire religious system has been known long since as Lamaism. The Kagyu-pa are also called "the White Sect." Some say this is because white was often worn by the founding fathers; others point to the fact that the walls of Kagyu-pa monasteries are painted white.

The Kagyu-pa trace their origins back to the famous Indian teacher and saint Ti-lo-pa, who is believed by the faithful to have been instructed, through celestial revelations, by the cosmic Buddha Vajradhara. Ti-lo-pa's main disciple, Na-ro-pa, passed on the mystical lore to Marpa (1012–1098), the first Tibetan in the succession.

Marpa and his pupil Milarepa, "Mila the Cotton-clad" (1040–1123), are two of the most eminent and extraordinary figures in the whole of Tibetan history. Fortunately the Western reader can follow without difficulty the stormy friendship between master and pupil through the pages of a classic biography of Milarepa by his contemporary Rechung (1084–1161), translated into English by W. J. Evans-Wentz and into French by Jacques Bacot (see Bibliography). The *Hundred Thousand Songs* by Milarepa, a mystic and a poet, have also been translated into English, by G. C. C. Chang. It is therefore possible to approach very closely these major figures of a brilliant and creative time in Tibetan spiritual history—the time of "the rising of Buddhism from the embers"—and to breathe the atmosphere in which they lived.

Milarepa had twenty-one disciples, among whom Rechung, his biographer, and Gampopa (1079–1153) were the most famous. Their pupils in turn founded a number of different schools. By the thirteenth century the genealogical tree of the Kagyu-pa sect had become very complicated, and it would take us too long to follow such developments in detail. Be it enough to say that three religious bodies of great importance in subsequent history were originally branches of the vigorous Kagyu stem: the Pagdru, or Phamo Drupa, the Karma-pa, and the Druk-pa. The first held a position of religious and political dominance in central Tibet during the fourteenth century, succeeding in secular power to the lamas of Sakya. The second—divided into two sections, "the Black Hats" and "the Red Hats"—became very strong in Tsang (Gyantse, Shigatse), opposing desperately the spread of the reformed Gelug-pa sect, from which the Dalai Lamas have come, during most of the fifteenth century. As for the Druk-pa, their moment of power came later, in the seventeenth century, when they founded an independent theocracy in what is now Bhutan.

Kagyu-pa teachings, common to all the many subsects, are derived mainly from the Indian teacher Na-ro-pa, and are essentially of a Tantric nature. Secret doctrines, giving allegedly mystical and magic powers, are passed orally from master to pupil, often with the aid of symbolic gestures, words, rituals, music, and images. The luxuriant nature of such symbolism is vividly represented by much of Tibetan religious art.

The Kadam-pa and *Gelug-pa* teachings can be traced back to Atisha and his disciple Drom Tonpa. Atisha insisted on a return to Buddha's original teachings and the observance of monastic discipline, and frowned upon the coarser forms of Tantric worship which had become so popular among the Tibetans. Atisha's pupils formed the Kadam-pa sect, from "kadam," which means "Buddha's teachings." With time, however, even the Kadam-pa sect lost much of its original purity and austerity: on the one hand there was the usual temptation of Tantrism, with its practice of exorcism and magic, and on the other there were the temptations of worldly power and political leadership.

An exceptionally gifted man appeared at this point and devoted his entire life to a reform of the Kadam-pa sect; this was Tsongkhapa (1357–1419), "He from the Onion Country," born on the northern borders of Tibet but educated in the central part of the country. His learning, his industry, his insight, and his dedication gained him many supporters, and he was able, while still very young, to gain a position of influence which permitted him to carry out a wide range of reforms.

Tsongkhapa looked back to Atisha and gave much importance to strict monastic discipline, requiring his followers to remain celibate and to abstain from intoxicating liquors; he was also a born organizer and leader of men, and under his guidance the Kadam-pa were reborn as the Gelug-pa, "the Virtuous Ones," a monastic order with a strict hierarchical structure. The Gelug-pa teachings required a gradual and parallel progress in moral integrity and intellectual excellence. The study of logic was considered very important, and monks took part in regular debates formalized according to rigorous rules. The Tantric aspects of Buddhism were not completely excluded, but initiations were accessible only to those well advanced along the path toward perfection. Gelug-pa ritual and garments soon acquired a character of their own; the followers of Tsongkhapa were to be known as "Yellow Caps" for the golden color of their headdress.

In 1409 Tsongkhapa, with the support of the leader of the Pagdru (Phamo Drupa) sect, organized the first great joint prayer service (Monlam) in Lhasa; Tsongkhapa also founded, that same year, the first Gelug-pa monastery, Gandan—so called from the name of the paradise of Maitreya, Buddha of the future age. A few years later (1416) one of his most prominent disciples, Thashi Panten, better known as Jamyang Choje, "Noble of the Law" (1379–1449) founded the Drepung Monastery in the western outskirts of Lhasa. The Sera Monastery, to the north of the capital, was founded in 1419 by another great disciple of Tsongkhapa, Jamchen Choje, known also as Sakya Yeshe. And by the middle of the sixteenth century many other monasteries of the Gelug-pa sect had been added to these three first and principal ones, in all parts of Tibet. Buddhism had never been so flourishing. No organized Buddhist sect had ever had so great a following as the Gelug-pa.

A principle of great consequence for its future development came into operation shortly after the time of Tsongkhapa; this was the tulku, "living Buddha," system, according to which the pontiffs of the Gelug-pa sect were believed to be successive incarnations of the Bodhisattva Chenresi, or Avalokitesvara, patron and protector of Tibet. The pontiffs of the once powerful Sakya sect had solved the problem of succession through marriage and family inheritance, those of the Kagyu-pa through the transmission of secret doctrines to chosen disciples. The Gelup-pa sect, having adopted celibacy and given more importance to rational thought and open teaching than to esoteric lore, would have found transmission of supreme authority from generation to generation a real problem, especially in a society unaccustomed to elections, had its leaders not relied on the idea of succession by reincarnation.

With Gedun Truppa (1391–1474), Tsongkhapa's successor as supreme Gelug-pa authority, and more so with Gedun Truppa's successors Gedun Gyatso (1475–1542) and Sonam Gyatso (1543–1588), the Gelug-pa became a powerful religious organization with burgeoning political ambitions. Sonam Gyatso invited the Mongol chief Altan Khan to descend on Tibet and force into submission rival sects actively supported by the kings of Tsang. Altan Khan accepted the invitation, marched into Tibet with his forces in 1578, defeated the opposition, and bestowed upon Sonam Gyatso the title of Dalai Lama ("Master Ocean of Wisdom"), by which he and his successors would be universally known; later on the title was made retroactive, so that Gedun Truppa and Gedun Gyatso became the First and Second Dalai Lamas.

The situation remained confused for another sixty years. In the meanwhile there had been a Fourth Dalai Lama, Yonten Gyatso (1589–1617), followed by the "Great Fifth" Dalai, Ngawang Lozang Gyatso (1617–1682). The Great Fifth was not only an outstanding scholar but a shrewd leader of men. Making deft use of another ambitious Mongol chief, Gushri Khan, he finally managed to have the kingdom of Tsang totally defeated. Tibet was now completely united. In 1642 Gushri Khan delegated the actual government of the country to the Fifth Dalai Lama, retaining for himself a role of military protector. These events are generally acknowledged to mark the actual birth of the Tibetan theocracy, under the Dalai Lamas of "the Yellow Sect," as it has been known up to our days. It had been a slow and circuitous process in which religious reform, missionary zeal, and growing political ambitions had finally been crowned by phenomenal success. In a sort of ceremonial climax of this achievement, during the years 1652 and 1653 the Fifth Dalai Lama visited Emperor Shun Zhi, fourth of the Manchu dynasty, in Beijing, where he was received with the highest honors.

The Great Fifth was also responsible for other decisions which turned Tibet into a country unique for its organization—and for its beauty. He had the majestic Potala Palace built, on the ruins of an ancient residence and castle of the Tibetan kings. As a gesture of gratitude to his teacher, abbot of the large monastery at Trashilungpo, near Shigatse, the Fifth Dalai Lama gave him the title of Panchen Rimpoche, "Precious Great Scholar." Since then the Trashilungpo abbots, the Panchen Lamas, have succeeded one another according to the principle of reincarnation followed by the Lhasa pontiffs. The Panchen Lamas are considered to be the incarnations of the supreme Buddha Amitabha (in Tibetan, Opame, "Boundless Light") who presides over our era, or kalpa, the fourth of the five composing the totality of cosmic history.

The Fifth Dalai Lama, the greatest ruler Tibet had known since ancient times, made full use of the political power he gained to extend the influence of the Yellow Sect, until it acquired complete supremacy over all other sects. By now it was the strongest in terms of its monastic institutions and the organization of its clergy. As these institutions were of such general importance to Tibet, we will here give a brief description of them:

The vast monasteries of Drepung (at one time over 8,000 monks), Sera (5,500), and Gandan (4,000) were organized into three groups known as the Lachi ("Cathedral"), Dratshang or Tatshang ("Theological College"), and Khamtshen ("Provincial Eating Club," which grouped the monks according to territorial origins and dialect). The Lachi, sometimes called Tsogchen ("the Great Chapter House"), was the main assembly hall of the monastery and center of all its activities at the highest level. It was run by a committee of Khanpo, or heads of Tatshang, and presided over by a lama of utmost seniority. Under the committee were several Chisos, or Chagdos, responsible for the management of all the Lachi's properties, including estates with houses and serfs attached to them, as well as trading, money lending, and other administrative and financial affairs; two Zhengo, responsible for the maintenance of order and discipline among the congregations and the trial of important cases among the lay population within the jurisdiction of the monastery; and a Tsogchen Umdse, who led the recitation of the sutras. Incumbents for the posts of Chagdos and Zhengo were recommended by the Khanpo and appointed by the Tibetan government.

At the second level was the Tatshang, the very nucleus of the organization of the monastery. Head of the Tatshang was a Khanpo, or abbot, who not only was responsible for everything pertaining to the monastery but also had a say in certain important government decisions. The Khanpo of all three leading monasteries was appointed by the Tibetan government from among the more eminent monks who had attained the exalted degree of Geshe. Under the Khanpo was the Labrang Chagdos, who with several assistants was responsible for the general administration, finance, and government of the whole lay population within the jurisdiction of the monastery as well as external relations. Next in order came the Gekor, the chief provost marshal, who kept the register of all members of the community, maintained discipline, and settled internal disputes; the Umdse, who led the chanting of the sacred scriptures; and a Zhunglaipa, who assisted the Khanpo in supervising the monks' studies and their examination for the exalted degree of Geshe. Appointment of all the above functionaries lay within the authority of the Khanpo.

The lowest level of the organization was the Khamtshen, a basic unit run by an executive committee under the chairmanship of a senior lama called the Khamtshen Gegen. Under him were a Nyerpa deputed to take care of property and funds, a Chinyer attending to the food, fuel, and other prime necessities of the community, and an Umdse, who presided at the prayer services. All these functionaries were elected by the committee members.

In such large monastic bodies as these the members were grouped according to occupations, like people anywhere. For example, there were the Choney and Ngapa to cater to the religious needs of the general public in times of sickness, birth, marriage, and death, and to the more primitive needs for fortune telling, performance of rites for bringing good luck, and the propitiation of evil forces. Then there were the monks specializing in medicine, astronomy, painting, sculpture, and the casting of images of Buddha. There were even monks who did only manual labor or acted as bodyguards or "muscle men." And then there were the scholar-monks who devoted themselves to the study of Buddhist scriptures in the hope of attaining the degree of Geshe. Khanpos, Chagdos, and other high functionaries in charge of the monasteries made up about 4 percent of the total; the rest were ordinary monks mostly from poor families. For many of the latter, entering a lamasery was their only way of escaping the direst poverty; many others were fugitives from forced labor or from usurers.

Religious education varied from sect to sect, but that of the Gelug-pa monasteries was the most comprehensive and systematic. In all the larger Gelug-pa establishments, separate schools with different curricula were provided for the normal and for the Tantric studies, though the former always came first. The general curriculum consisted of five basic courses, including dialectics, disciplinary rules, and principal doctrines. It took a scholar-monk about twenty years to finish the course and qualify to sit for the examination for the degree of Geshe. After gaining this degree, he might enter the Gyupa academy, where he might immerse himself in Tantric studies for decades before possibly attaining the highest honor, that of becoming Gandan Khripa and occupying the throne of Tsongkhapa in the Gandan Monastery.

Lastly let me add a few words about the religious festivals of Tibet. There are a great many of them. On these occasions services are held in chapels or monasteries from dawn till dusk, and the faithful come there to pray amid the chanting of sutras and the burning of incense, giving alms and replenishing butter lamps that burn before the altar. Some of the main festivals concerned strictly with the Buddha are, according to the Tibetan calendar, April 15, Buddha's birthday; February 15, the day of his death; and June 4, the occasion of his first sermon in the park at Benares.

The great master Tsongkhapa died in 1419, the day of his death being November 25 according to the Tibetan calendar. This day has ever after been set apart by all followers of the Gelug-pa sect for a special annual service in his memory. Then, besides the religious ceremonies and prayers that take place in all Yellow Sect monasteries, hundreds and even thousands of small butter lamps are lit on the roofs as evening falls, as offerings in his memory. This is commonly called "the night of the lamp offering."

Apart from these festivals, all monasteries hold "retreats" in both summer and winter, and for periods of one or two months the lamas devote themselves to reading the holy scriptures and debating theological matters. These are also occasions for devout Buddhists to visit holy places and perform charitable and worthy deeds.

It is now well over a thousand years since Buddhism was introduced to Tibet, and throughout this time the influence of Buddhist belief on the people of Tibet has been profound and all-embracing. Whether in the cities or in the remoter country districts, the majority of Tibetans today are still devout Buddhists.

120. *Sakyamuni—the Buddha, or Enlightened One. As most Tibetans are Buddhists, the image of Sakyamuni is to be seen almost everywhere in Tibet. This famous statue in the Tsulhakhang Temple, or Jokhang, in Lhasa is traditionally believed to have been brought by Princess Wen Cheng from Changan in the seventh century.*

122

121. *The great Buddhist reformer Tsongkhapa Lozang Drakpa, was born in 1357 at Tsongkha in the province of Qinghai. Coming to central Tibet at the age of sixteen, he learned from the doctrines of all the Buddhist sects and became the founder of the Gelug-pa, or "Yellow Sect." He built the Gandan Monastery. Gandan and the Drepung and Sera monasteries, founded by his disciples, became the three leading monasteries of the Gelug-pa sect.*

122. *A fresco in a corridor on the top floor of the Sakya Monastery, showing one of the early leaders of the Sakya sect. The high lamas of this sect ruled over Tibet for almost 100 years while the Mongols were in the ascendancy in the thirteenth and fourteenth centuries.*

123. *The figure on the right is Ngawang Lozang Gyatso (1617–1682), the Fifth Dalai Lama and one of the truly great rulers in Tibetan history. He paid a visit to the emperor of the Qing dynasty in 1652 and 1653, receiving a gold seal and diploma together with an honorific title. He kept a firm hand on both the political and religious affairs of Tibet, and under him the country's theocracy was enormously strengthened.*

124. *Throughout Tibet, where the majority of the people are Buddhists, images of the Buddha in all sizes can be seen carved or painted on stones on the hilltops or walls beside the roads.*

125. No fewer than 20,000 volumes of Buddhist scriptures are preserved in the great library of the Sakya Monastery. The photo shows a priceless codex all written in letters of gold. Its dimensions are 5.6 by 4.3 by 3.3 feet.

126. A copy of the Mahaprajnaparamita Sutra written in gold letters. It is preserved in the Potala Palace in Lhasa.

127. Buddhist scriptures written on patra (palm) leaves from ancient India. Now a great rarity, specimens are preserved in the Potala Palace and the Sakya and Trashilungpo monasteries.

128

129

128. *The wood-block printing press and library at Derge on the Tibet-Sichuan boundary are the largest of their kind on the Tibetan tableland. Vast numbers of engraved wooden boards are preserved there, including Buddhist scriptures and works on Tibetan history, literature, medicine, astronomy, and astrology. The photo shows printing actually in progress.*

129. *Lamas—Tibetan Buddhist monks—reading the Buddhist canon.*

130. *The systematic checking and cataloguing of Tibetan Buddhist works.*

131. *In the Tibetan calendar the fourth of June is the anniversary of the Buddha's first sermon. Solemn services are held in all monasteries, with prayers and the chanting of sutras by the light of hundreds of butter lamps. This photo was taken at the Sera Monastery.*

132. *Lamas on the steps of a monastery in southeastern Tibet.*

134

135

133. *Churning butter for tea, the traditional beverage of Tibet.*

134. *A corner in a lamasery kitchen. In the past, some of the largest monasteries had to cater for up to 8,000 lamas.*

135. *Fetching water, one of the menial tasks traditionally relegated to trapa, or junior monks, in addition to the performance of their spiritual duties.*

136

137

136. *One of the tasks of lamas has traditionally been to prepare torma, conical cakes made of tsampa (roasted gingke flour and butter), for placement on the altar or use in rituals.*

137. *Dusting holy images.*

138. *Adding butter to lamps while they are burning. In Tibet butter is a product of prime importance, not only in diet but for use as fuel and even for making images of the Buddha.*

140

141

139. *A lama eating the roasted, buttered gingke flour called tsampa in his room. Gingke, the staple food of Tibet, is a particularly hardy kind of highland barley.*

140. *Playing sho, a popular game using dice.*

141. *The drinking of buttered tea forms a part of numerous ancient customs in Tibet.*

142. *A Buddhist nun, her head shaven, holding a prayer wheel in one hand and prayer beads in the other.*

143

144

143. *Seated on the ground at the foot of the Potala Palace, this devout Buddhist is softly reciting holy scriptures.*

144. *A bookseller hawking his wares in the street. Most of what he sells will be designed to appeal to Buddhist pilgrims.*

145. *Devout Tibetan Buddhists regard the Potala as inhabited by divine power. People still observe the old rule of walking only at the very edge of the staircase. Prostrate in the foreground is a pilgrim displaying the most devout form of obeisance.*

146. *Standing before a temple, this believer holds a prayer wheel in one hand and prayer beads in the other.*

Chapter VII   Palaces, Monasteries, and Their Art

147. *The thirteen-story Potala Palace of today is 386.73 feet in height, and is a spectacle of grandeur from 6 miles away.*

Dongge Luosantselie

If you were to stand on the summit of Mount Chomolungma, known in the west as Mount Everest and quite literally the roof of the world, you would be rewarded with a bird's-eye view of the vast expanse of land that is Tibet, awesomely beautiful with its snow-capped mountains and dense forests. This is the landscape in which the Tibetan people have grown and thrived for generation after generation, century after century, and which is the most cherished treasure of our motherland. In this landscape, over thousands of years, our ancestors have built a history that we are proud of, and have with their own hands fashioned a culture both rich and unique. By way of illustration, from the architecture of our monasteries and palaces we can get some idea of the splendors of Tibetan art, an art that affects the viewer like the running of a stream of clear water.

In the macaque-monkey caves at Tsethang in the Yarlung valley and in the southern forests of Pomed and Kongpo we find traces of the cave and "nest" dwellers who were our remote ancestors. Along the eastern stretch of the Yarlung Tsangpo River and at Karo village in the region of Chamdo, traces of primitive communities have recently been discovered. The earliest Tibetan buildings, the "nests" of the nest dwellers, had a wooden post in the center buttressed by smaller posts on all sides, and a roof made of wood and bamboo shafts and straw mats plastered with mud and grass. The technique was based on the arrangement of a bird's feathers, with the top layer overlapping the layer beneath. The earliest wood and stone building in Tibet was the palace beside the Yarlung Tsangpo River built for the Tibetan king Nyatri Tsenpo, who according to the traditional dates lived some 2,000 years ago. It is a five-story fortress-like dwelling known as the Yumbu Lagang. The inner walls of the palace were once adorned with frescoes recording the enthronement of the Tsenpo and the acclamations of the people, and telling stories illustrating the Bon religion.

Three of the most magnificent ancient buildings erected between the seventh and ninth centuries, approximately from the reign of Songtsen Gampo to the heyday of Lang Darma of the Yarlung Dynasty, have been preserved to this day. Each deserves a full description.

The Tsulhakhang Temple. Songtsen Gampo had this temple built to welcome Bhrikuti Devi, the Nepalese princess whom he took to wife. The front gate faced toward her native land. The walls were built of brick. The crossbeams, columns, and corbels were installed in a style that reflects a mixture of the Tibetan and the Nepalese. The roof was tiled, as was the custom in inner Tibet. Later on the roofs of the Sakyamuni and Avalokitesvara halls were covered with gold, and with the accession of the Sixth Dalai Lama (who was also a famous poet) golden roofs replaced all the conventional ones. In 1409 the Pagdru king Drakpa Gyaltsen built an extension in front of the Gate of the Lion's Head at Tsulhakhang. The regent Sangye Gyatso, who died around 1705, added new halls, and many more buildings were erected in and around the reign of the Eighth Dalai Lama and the temple acquired more or less the scale that we see today.

The Samye Monastery. In the latter half of the eighth century King Trisong Detsen invited the Indian Buddhist teachers Padmasambhava (in Tibetan, Guru Rimpoche) and Santarakshita to come to Yarlung and preach the Law, and in about 779 he had the Samyé Monastery built according to the plan and scale of the Otantapuri Monastery in India. Indian-style wooden structures were used for the third and top floors in homage to India as the source of Buddhism, while the middle floor used the typical Chinese brick structure. Stone was used for the ground floor to signify the spreading of the Buddhist Law throughout the land of Tibet—a symbol like the rock of St. Peter. The soaring eaves and roofbeams on each floor were in the Chinese architectural style, and the roofs were covered with tiles. There are twelve Buddhist halls in the monastery, the imperial consorts having commissioned one each. The compound also contains Buddhist chortens, and a word on these typical structures may be useful here.

A chorten ("chorten" is a Tibetan word meaning "receptable for offerings") is normally a solid conical masonry structure from 3 to 30 feet high, or even higher. It may contain the remains of holy men, sacred books, images, or offerings of any kind. It is derived ultimately from the Indian stupa, a solid, simple, massive dome of masonry constructed for religious purposes, and commenorates the monument in which the Buddha's ashes were buried. Chortens are representations of the Buddhist universe, and every part of the structure has a precise and subtly symbolic meaning. In this monastery the chortens are colored in white, red, black, and blue, and no fewer than 108 of them stand around the walls.

The Ushangdo Chapel. This monastery on the lower reaches of the Lhasa River (Kyi-chu) was founded by King Tride Songtsen at the beginning of the ninth century. It has nine stories, the upper three being made of wood and devoted entirely to Buddhist images, scriptures, and chortens. The middle three floors are built of brick, and the lower three are of mud and stone.

The Potala Palace in Lhasa, one of the most majestic buildings in the whole of Asia, has a special history. It is related that the seventh-century king Songtsen Gampo chose the plains of Rasa, "the Goat Land," as his residence, and that the place later became known as Lhasa, "the God's Land." On a steep hill north of the plains a large palace was built; it was said to resemble a sleeping elephant, and was called "the white royal residence." The king enlarged this palace to please his royal consorts coming from distant lands, and it is said that it was eventually nine stories high and contained 900 rooms. After the first Tibetan kingdom ended in 842, its various monumental buildings fell into decay, and not much of the ancient palace can have been left when the Fifth Dalai Lama, the great Ngawang Lozang Gyatso, started in 1642 to construct the vast "Buddhist Vatican" that we see today.

As discussed in Chapter VI, "Tibetan Buddhism," King Lang Darma attempted to wipe out Buddhism in Tibet, and to some extent he succeeded. It was not until some 150 years after his assassination in 842 that the country underwent a great Buddhist revival. The three centuries that followed saw a boom in the construction of temples and monasteries, keeping pace with the development of the various Buddhist sects. The temples were places of worship, the monasteries the religious communities that surrounded them. The most important and representative monasteries from this period are:

The Toling Monastery, built by a king of Guge who became a monk, Lho Lama Yeshe-Ö, in 996.

The Thangpoche Monastery, built by Drume Tshukhrim Chungne in 1011.

The Reting Monastery, built by Drom Tonpa in 1056.

The first monastery of the Sakya sect, built by Khon Konchog Gyalpo in 1073.

The Sangphu Monastery, built by Lekpa Sherab in 1073.

The Zhalu Monastery, built by Sherab Chungne in 1087.

The Narthang Monastery, built by Lodro Drapa in 1153.

When Tibet came into the sphere of influence of the Yuan dynasty, the Sakya and Kagyu-pa sects enjoyed special favor with the Mongols. It was during this period that the great Sakya Monastery and the Taklung, Drikhung, and Riwoche monasteries were built.

King Drakpa Gyaltsen, fifth of the Pagdru dynasty (1350–1442), had the most profound reverence for the buddhist teacher and reformer Tsongkhapa (1357–1419), with the result that monasteries of his Gelug-pa sect proliferated. These included:

The Gandan Monastery, built by Tsongkhapa in 1409.

The Drepung Monastery, built by Jamyang Choje, a disciple of Tsongkhapa, in 1416.

The Sera Monastery, built by Jamchen Choje, another disciple of Tsongkhapa, in 1419.

The Palchor Monastery, built by the religious lord of Gyantse, Rabten Kunzang Phagpa, between 1414 and 1424.

The great chorten of the Palchor Monastery at Gyantse, built by Phagpa Rinchen in 1439. The chorten is also known as the Kum-Bum, "the Hundred Thousand," on account of its many images.

The Chamdo Monastery, built by Mai Jangsem Sherab, another of Tsongkhapa's disciples, in 1444.

The Trashilungpo Monastery, built by the First Dalai Lama, Gedun Truppa, in 1447.

Thus over a period of less than half a century, while the Gelug-pa sect was in the ascendant, many famous Buddhist shrines were completed, all of them majestic, on a grand scale, and embodying the very essence of Tibetan architecture. The great chorten of the Palchor Monastery at Gyantse, for example, is a perfect six-story building, complete with a Buddhist Hall and a prayer hall. Its seventy-three chapels contain a very important cycle of religious paintings. But the most magnificent and famous building in Tibet remains the Potala Palace, particularly since it was rebuilt by the Fifth Dalai Lama and the regent Sangye Gyatso. The work of an army of craftsmen in every field, it is surely one of the wonders of the world.

The monasteries and palaces of Tibet themselves display the unique features of our country's art. All of them, from the Potala Palace to the most humble monastery, are composed of a number of buildings at various levels so as to conform to the terrain. Though orderly, symmetrical, stately, and imposing, they are entirely free of any sense of rigidity. Their dressed stone, their Chinese-style golden roofs and stacked eaves, and their Indian-influenced wooden structures are fused effortlessly into an artistic whole. So naturally do these diverse features combine that the Tibetan style emerges as perfectly distinct. Moreover, every palace or monastery is a treasure-house of Tibetan Buddhist art, glowing with the rare and precious works of anonymous artists throughout the centuries.

Tibetans traditionally classify their Buddhist works of art into kuten (body), sungten (language), and chorten (meaning)—and indeed all chortens do contain a meaning symbolized by their very forms. The chorten is of course a material structure. In concrete terms "kuten" refers to Buddhist images, "sungten" to Buddhist scriptures. A Tibetan monastery is treasured and revered by the common people precisely because it houses and safeguards these three manifestations of art, among which, however, the Buddhist image embodies the highest artistic achievement.

Kuten: Buddhist Images. There are ten different kinds of Buddhist images, distinguished mainly according to the materials used:

1. **Cast metal statues.** These may be cast in gold, silver, or bronze. The best-known Buddhist statues are those cast in a special alloy of gold, silver, bronze, and tin. Their dimensions vary from the monumental to life-size and down to the size of a finger. Among the celebrated cast statues are those of Sakyamuni, the Buddha, at the Tsulhakhang Temple, or Jokhang, which contains 13,613 taels of pure gold (20,419 ounces—a tael equals one and a half ounces); the statues of Padmasambhava, Tsongkhapa, and the Fifth Dalai Lama preserved in the Khrungrub Lhakang Hall in the Potala Palace, each containing 1,246 taels of pure gold (1,869 ounces); and the five-story-high statue of Maitreya at the Trashilungpo Monastery. All are priceless examples of Tibetan workmanship.

2. **Clay statues.** The clay statue is the most common kind of Buddhist image, and no Tibetan monastery would be complete without an example. During the long development of Tibetan Buddhism the techniques of other nations were gradually assimilated to form a style of molding clay that is uniquely Tibetan. At the beginning of the eleventh century the emergence of various Buddhist sects and the consequent boom in the construction of monasteries and temples led to enormous demand for this type of statue. The Narthang, Sakya, Reting, Dakla Gampo, Zhalu, and Sangphu monasteries are outstanding for their collections of statues and images of all kinds, of Buddhas both enthroned and realistic, dignified and awe-inspiring. This period was a turning point in the modeling of clay statues, an art in which Tibetans attained the highest possible level.

3. **Carved wooden statues.** The carved statues of Sakyamuni that in the seventh century were brought to Songtsen Gampo from the Tang court and from Nepal have been preserved intact to this day. They bear witness to an art of wood carving that can be traced to a number of different sources. Not only statues but also engravings in wood and wood blocks for printing display the most consummate skill. Famous examples are the set of thirty-five engravings made in the reign of the Seventh Dalai Lama, narrating the story of Bodhisattvas practicing asceticism to assuage the sufferings of mankind, and the *Complete Works of Tsongkhapa,* which were preserved in the Gandan Monastery. The carving of columns is a branch of this same art, and in the Tsulhakhang Temple certain columns are named after the carvings on them:

Tea Leaf, Magic Urn, Lion, Snakehead, and so on. These wonderful examples of the wood carver's art also date from the reign of Songtsen Gampo.

4. Carved stone statues. Stone carving in Tibet is of two kinds, bas-relief and engraving. Bas-relief is practiced on rocky mountainsides, examples being the images of the sixteen Arhats, whereas engravings of various kinds can be found on cliff faces all over Tibet. The art of stone carving in this country goes back over a thousand years. The famous "doring" of Tibet, such as the tablet erected to mark the founding of the Samye Monastery in the eighth century, is not only testimony to the growth of Buddhism in Tibet, but proof of the long standing of Tibetan stone carving as well. In fact, the word "doring" (literally "long stone") refers not only to such relatively sophisticated works as this but also to the prehistoric rude monoliths called "menhirs" which are often found in the country. Even in the remotest places, where one might well think man's foot had never trod, one is astonished to find scriptural incantations of every kind, in various patterns and styles of writing, carved on a rock beside a goat path or on a cliff face.

5. Buddhist images painted on satin. We find written records of these as early as the beginning of the sixteenth century. In the mid-seventeenth century Gushri Khan gave the Fifth Dalai Lama a satin image that is still preserved in the Potala Palace. Many such works are found in monasteries such as Drepung and Trashilungpo. Some of them are as high as a three-story building.

6. Images made by the appliqué, or "clip and paste," method. Collages of this kind are mostly done on silk and satin and decorated with jewels and tassels. Just such an image hangs on the Long Column in the stupa hall of the Fifth Dalai Lama in the Potala Palace.

7. Frescoes. Wall painting is the oldest form of painting in Tibet. Ancient historical documents record that Songtsen Gampo, while seated in meditation at Lhasa, saw a wall painting on the cliff face opposite him. The Chamdo Monastery has frescoes depicting early Tibetans making charcoal, opening up virgin land, bridging rivers, and so on. Frescoes at the eighth-century Samye Monastery show the ceremonies that took place at the inauguration of the monastery, as well as incidents from the wars between the kings of Yarlung and the Tang emperors of China. Outstanding examples of this form of art are the fifteenth-century frescoes in the great chorten of the Palchor Monastery at Gyantse, mentioned above. Dating from shortly after the pagoda was completed, these "hundred thousand images" (actually 27,529 according to one count), include, as might be expected, a number of almost mechanical repetitions of obscure Buddhist deities, of both the benign and "terrific" varieties. But very many of these paintings, and particularly the larger ones, are of the highest artistic value, and what is more are in a magnificent state of preservation. Interestingly enough, though the major influence on these paintings is still Indian, quite a number show evident Chinese influence, particularly in the landscapes in the background and in the portraits of donors of the frescoes.

8. Buddhist images on cloth, or thangkas. This is the best known of all forms of Tibetan painting. Even in the West the Tibetan word "thangka" is sometimes used to denote this form of painting, which may perhaps have been of Indian origin but became a specialty in Tibet. A thangka supposedly executed in the blood of Songtsen Gampo himself at a time when he had a nosebleed is said to be concealed inside a statue in the Tsulhakhang Temple. During Atisha's lifetime his disciple Nagtso Lotsawa painted a portrait of him on cloth, with Atisha himself in the center surrounded by his most illustrious disciples. At the bottom is a brief life of this great teacher, while on the back are written eighteen eulogistic poems.

9. **Tibetan "gouache."** In this technique an outline is first sketched on a board or even on the ground. White stone is then powdered and mixed with pigments, and the mixture is forced into a kind of iron tube resembling a fountain pen. A gentle shaking movement is used to trace out what are called "Lhoka Chojungs," some of them as big as a room, others scarcely smaller than a foot in length. This kind of painting was developed in Tibet during the eleventh century. Works of this kind are specially made for the festivals held four times a year to maintain general awareness of the Buddhist Law. They comprise a unique art form that calls for outstanding sensitivity and complete mastery on the part of the artist. However, it has one serious drawback: works done by this method are extremely hard to preserve.

10. **Kneading colored butter.** Statues are made by mixing butter with pigments and molding the mixture into the desired shapes. The finished work is then mounted on a specially designed board or put in a wooden box for viewing. Because of our highland climate these colored-butter statues can be kept for years without deteriorating. At the four great festivals, and especially at the Dharma Meeting on January 15 by the Tibetan calender, a vast number of such images are put on show. Themes are taken either from the Buddhist scriptures or from Tibetan operas. A work made of colored butter may be three stories high or as tiny as an ant. This traditional art is peculiarly Tibetan and enjoys widespread popularity. Artists are trained in this technique in numerous monasteries and elsewhere, and study sessions for practitioners of the art are organized from time to time.

The visual artforms described above are considered the highest and most spectacular of the three great Buddhist arts.

Sungten: Buddhist Scriptures. Tibetan sungtens are Buddhist classic scriptures. Sungtens are kept by every monastery in the country, to be read and chanted by every monk. At the same time they are masterpieces of Buddhist art.

There are two main types of sungten: handwritten and block-printed. Both forms are typically Tibetan, and are far more than ordinary books.

The earliest sungtens were of course handwritten. They came into being in the early seventh century along with the Tibetan written language. This was evolved by Thonmi Sambhota by adaping various Indian alphabets current at the time. Tibetan script is therefore phonetic, and not ideographic like the Chinese form of writing. There are forty signs, all read in conjunction with the vowel "a" ("ka," "kha," "sa," "sha," etc.); other vowels are indicated by small signs written above or below the consonants. Reading and writing Tibetan is very difficult because over the centuries the spelling has largely remained the same, while the pronunciation has evolved, mostly toward simpler solutions. The same problem, of course, is characteristic of English.

One of the treasures that has survived from ancient times is the Buddhist canon written on patra (palm) leaves; examples can be found in a handful of monasteries, but they are extremely rare. The texts were sometimes written in Sanskrit, sometimes in old Tibetan. The leading monasteries of the various sects all have complete sets of the 108-volume *Kangyur* scriptures, handwritten in gold and held to be masterpieces of the calligrapher's art. Some are particularly celebrated, such as the five sets written in gold, silver, copper, iron, and cinnabar by order of the regent Sangye Gyatso after the death of the Fifth Dalai Lama. At the time of the Tenth Dalai Lama the Religious Lord Pholuoding sponsored the copying of the *Kangyur* in letters of liquid gold. This set was later presented to the Gandan Monastery and is now preserved in the Potala Palace. At the Trashilungpo Monastery the Fifth and Sixth Panchen Lamas each sponsored a set of the Buddhist canon, one in gold and the other in silver.

According to Tibetan records, block-printed editions of the sungten began to be produced in the late thirteenth century. It is mainly due to the development and popularity of block printing that the *Kangyur* and *Tangyur* scriptures, two famous sungtens compiles in Tibetan under the direction of Buton Rimpoche (1290–1364) in the Zhalu Monastery, have survived intact until the present day. The highest level in the art of printing is held to have been reached by the Narthang and Trashilungpo monasteries, and by the Buddhist Scripture Printing House in Lhasa. Each of these centers has a number of experts who are not only skilled in block printing but outstanding also in the interpretation of the scriptures. Moreover, each center has its distinctive style of printing.

The Chorten. The Tibetan chorten, another typical form of Buddhist art, can be made of various materials, including stone, mud brick, bronze, silver, and gold.

Stone chortens are the oldest kind. It is said that the five stone chortens behind the Chamdo Monastery in eastern Tibet were built under the sponsorship of Songtsen Gampo himself. The Palchor Monastery at Gyantse and the Champaling Monastery at Dranang have very large chortens renowned far and wide, and a gigantic chorten of the pagoda type is also to be seen at the monastery of Kum-Bum, in Qinghai where Tsongkhapa was born.

Chortens built of mud bricks are extremely rare. The one near the Zhalu Monastery was built under the auspices of Buton himself.

Bronze chortens are usually gilded, and famous for their exquisite workmanship.

Gold and silver chortens traditionally called stupas have been used to hold the remains of very high-ranking lamas. The two-story-high stupa of the Third Dalai Lama in the Drepung Monastery is made of silver. On either side of the mourning hall of the Fifth Dalai Lama stand eight chortens, each nearly three stories high; around 2,000 taels of silver (3,000 ounces) was employed on each of them.

The stupa of the Fifth Dalai Lama is plated with pure gold and weighs 119,082 taels (179,703 ounces). That of the Thirteenth Dalai Lama used over 10,000 taels (15,000 ounces) of gold. Both are inlaid with jewels and are in every sense priceless treasures.

As I myself am not an architect, let alone an artist, I am all too aware of the shortcomings of my presentation of the art of Tibet. But I am a native Tibetan and a man who loves learning, as I love my country and my own home town. Ever since I began to learn and to study sungtens in a monastery, I have been deeply interested in Buddhist art and have studied it as much as possible in its three manifestations as described above. Wherever I have lived and worked it has been part of me, and the longer I live, the more I come to appreciate the finer points of Tibetan Buddhist art. Here I have tried to convey it to you in the plainest terms possible. It is my most cherished hope that in reading this book you will come to understand and gain something from what has been achieved and made in my motherland through the centuries. To deserve our admiration and yours was the basic aim of the artists and architects who brought these treasures into being centuries ago. I hope that our art and our landscape will forge a link with people all over the world, for art is ever young, and a living thing.

I send my greetings to the reader and my thanks for his attention.

148. These steps and walls of granite blocks lead up to the gate of the Donang Hall in the Potala Palace.

149. The majestic Potala Palace rises on the Red Hill in Lhasa. The word "Potala" means "the holy abode of Avalokitesvara." A palace is said to have been built here by Songtsen Gampo in the seventh century. Later it fell into decay. A thousand years after Songtsen Gampo, the Fifth Dalai Lama started its rebuilding and extension as the Potala.

150. The golden roofs of the Potala are an emblem of the grandeur of the Buddha.

152

153

151. Halfway up the Red Hill is Devangshar Square, more than 230 feet above ground level and with an area of 17,400 square feet. Here the Dalai Lama would watch plays and dances on festive occasions.

152. The outer walls of the Potala Palace are several yards thick in places.

153. A rear view of the Potala.

154

155

154. The Potala has hundreds of rooms, and its corridors form a great labyrinth. Here is a corner with lavish decorations typical of the whole interior.

155. The East Hall in the eastern part of the Potala. Built in 1645, it is the largest hall in the whole palace. The installations of the Dalai Lamas and other important ceremonies traditionally have been held here. And since the late eighteenth century this room has witnessed the drawing of lots from the golden urn to decide in whom the Dalai Lama has been reincarnated when rival candidates have appeared.

156. Columns carved into typical Tibetan patterns.

158

159

157. A richly decorated lintel in the Potala Palace.

158. A stupa in the Potala Palace. The stupa is the final resting place for the remains of high-ranking lamas. Those of the Dalai Lamas are gold- or silver-plated and inlaid with precious stones.

159. The Pearl Tower in the stupa hall of the Thirteenth Dalai Lama. Inset with over 200,000 pearls, it is a priceless treasure of Tibetan art.

160. The Dalai Lama's bedchamber on the top floor of the White Palace in the Potala.

162

163

164

161. *This bronze doorknocker on one of the gates of the Potala is an exquisite example of the engraver's craft.*

162. *The stupa of the Eleventh Dalai Lama in the Potala Palace. There are eight stupas in the palace, uniform in style but of different sizes. The most elaborate belong to the Fifth and Thirteenth Dalai Lamas. The former is 49.2 feet high, and is plated with 119,802 taels of gold (179,703 ounces) and lavishly inlaid with pearls, precious stones, and amber.*

163. *Princess Jin Cheng, adopted daughter of Emperor Zhong Zong of the Tang dynasty. By her marriage in 710 to Tride Tsugtsen, she became the second Tang princess to marry a king of Yarlung. Along* with a small army of Chinese craftsmen, she brought with her musicians and such books as Classic Poetry as Annotated by Mao Chang, The Commentary of Tso, *and* Records of Rites. *Thus she stimulated the development of cultural and economic exchange between the Chinese and Tibetan peoples at that early date.*

164. *Decorative patterns on the base of a niche prepared for an image of the Buddha.*

165. *This fresco depicts a horserace and an archery competition on horseback, reminding us of the warlike pride of the Tibetans and their natural talents as horsemen. The frescoes in the Potala have the most diverse subjects, but in all of them the workmanship is supreme.*

ༀ༔ ཁྱི་ཕྱིང་གི་མེད་ལྕས་དཔལ་ཕུར་འེ་ གསལ་ རྫོ་མ་དིར་གས༔
མོན་པ་བསྐྲན་འཛོན་དེ། ཡེ་ལྒྱུ་བཙེར་ཉིས་ས་ཕྱུང་བ༔

166. The Tsulhakhang Temple in the middle of Lhasa, which became known as the Jokhang, is one of the oldest temples in Tibet; it was built in the seventh century under Songtsen Gampo to mark the arrival of Princess Bhrikuti Devi. With an area of 273,000 square feet, the main hall is a three-story buiding, and its golden-colored bronze-plated roof is characteristic of the Tibetan style of architecture. Statues of the Buddha (Sakyamuni), Songtsen Gampo, and the Princesses Wen Cheng and Bhrikut Devi are enshrined in the temple.

167. Another view of the Jokhang. The great bell-shaped object (gyamtschen) is a symbol of the flourishing of Buddhism.

168

169

228

168. *The golden roof of the Jokhang. The main ridge is decorated with urns, pearls, golden bells, and animals of cast metal. Dragons and hanging bells at the tips of the soaring eaves lend a touch of the style of Chinese monasteries to the overall architecture traditional to Tibet.*

170. *The Jokhang: statues of Songtsen Gampo, Princess Wen Cheng, and the king's Nepalese wife Bhrikuti Devi. Wen Cheng is in the foreground, Bhrikuti Devi in the background.*

169. *Gyamtschen, symbolic of the flourishing of Buddhism, are displayed on the rooftops of the Potala Palace and the Jokhang in Lhasa, the Trashilungpo Monastery in Shigatse, and Lhasa's famous Drepung and Sera monasteries.*

171

171. *The Avalokitesvara of the Thousand Hands and Eyes in the main hall of the Jokhang.*

172. *The bronze statue of Maitreya in the prayer hall of the Jokhang, standing 247.5 feet high. It was cast by the Tibetan government in 1736.*

174

*173/174. These frescoes on the third floor
of the Jokhang depict two goddesses who are
"guardians of the Law."*

175

234

176

175. The main hall of the Jokhang has a paneled ceiling, and the bracketed columns and crossbeams are embellished with human figures, animals, and birds, all either painted or carved in wood.

176. The entrance to the Norbu Lingka (Jewel Park), which lies southwest of the Potala and occupies an area of more than one and a fourth square miles. Modeled on the palace gardens of the Chinese emperors, it was built in the late eighteenth century. Today it is open to the public.

177. Chinese-style corbels at the Jokhang, the joint work of craftsmen brought by Princess Wen Cheng from China and Princess Bhrikuti Devi from Nepal.

178. The Drepung Monastery, built in 1416, is one of the great monasteries of Lhasa. The buildings, statues, and artistic treasures are all in a good state of preservation. At one time there were more than 8,000 monks in this monastery.

177

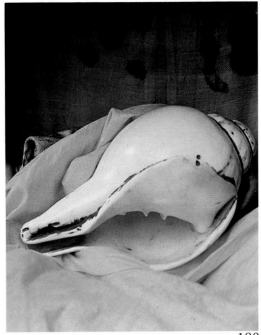

180

181

179. One of the main buildings in the Drepung Monastery.

180. Preserved in the Drepung Monastery, this conch—a symbol of succession like the keys of the kingdom—is said to have been unearthed by Tsong khapa in 1416 and given to his disciple Jamyang Choje Thashi Panten, founder of the Drepung Monastery, so that he would adhere to and turn the Wheel of Law.

181. Buddha Champa (Maitreya, Buddha of the future age), one of the earliest statues erected in the Drepung Monastery. Legend relates that this statue contains the golden saddle of a divine horse that once belonged to a certain Prince Zhonnu Dondru.

182. Hangings in the Drepung Monastery's main hall, which was traditionally used for meditation.

183. The Sera Monastery on the northern outskirts of Lhasa. One of the chief monasteries of the Yellow Sect, it was built in 1419. With an initial enrollment of 5,500 monks, it at once became one of the sect's three great monasteries.

184. Large Tibetan monasteries are built like towns. Here a lama is threading his way through the alleyways of the Sera Monastery.

185. The statue of Sakyamuni, the Buddha, in the Hall of Sixteen Arhats in the Sera Monastery. Jamchen Choje, a disciple of Tsongkhapa also known as Sakya Yeshe, was granted the title of Religious Lord of Great Mercy by Emperor Xuan Zong of the Ming dynasty of China. Among the presents the emperor gave him were sixteen Arhat statues carved from sandalwood, for the worship of which this hall was specially built.

186

186. Clay replicas of the sixteen Arhat statues presented to Jamchen Choje Sakya Yeshe by Emperor Xuan Zong of the Ming dynasty. They are said to have been molded on the original wooden statues.

187. An embroidered thangka (painted scroll) showing the empress of China worshipping Buddha and listening to the Buddhist scriptures, with glosses in Chinese. This too was a present to Jamchen Choje from Emperor Xuan Zong.

188. A fresco showing the Samye Monastery in a symbolic setting. The monastery consisted of 108 buildings built in the eighth century during the reign of Trisong Detsen.

假借四大以為身
心本無生因境有
前境若無心亦無
罪福如幻起亦滅

189

190

189. *The gatehouse of the enclosed courtyard of the Samye Monastery, showing many features typical of Tibetan religious buildings, including the sloping stone walls and the wooden structures above. Note also the furled symbolic umbrella, known as a kenchira, on the roof and the cloth hangings on the lintel. Umbrellas are placed over the heads of important lamas when they preach. Buddha is always seen under a sacred umbrella—sometimes more than one—when he is shown preaching.*

190. *A hall in the Samye Monastery.*

191. *Carved wooden decorations on a corbel in the Samye Monastery.*

192

192. The Tradru Temple near Tsethang in the Yarlung valley, built in the seventh century and later enlarged. Songtsen Gampo and Princess Wen Cheng once resided there, and in a side hall there is a cooking stove believed to have been used by the princess herself.

193. A fresco in a side hall of the Tradru Temple. The coloring and brushwork indicate a painting of the thirteenth century.

194. Ruins dating from the kingdom of Guge at Ngari in the upper Satlej valley in western Tibet. With an area of almost three-fourths of a square mile, the palace was built on a hill, the slope of which is dotted with 300 houses and 300 caves, in addition to the great Buddhist chortens in the foreground. The kingdom of Guge was founded around the tenth century, when the Yarlung dynasty was in decline.

193

195. *Frescoes from temple ruins dating back to the ancient kingdom of Guge, Ngari. Both colorful and realistic, they are mostly portraits of Buddhas and Bodhisattvas and the king and his ministers. Others depict dances and scenes from everyday life.*

196. *Coat of mail, shield, and arrows found in the ruins of the kingdom of Guge at Ngari.*

197

198

197. The Zhalu Monastery was built in 1087 in the Gyatso district some 12 miles from Shigatse. It reveals a mixture of the traditional Tibetan and Chinese styles. The great Tibetan scholar Buton was once abbot here.

198. Few of the yellow and green glazed tiles now remain on the roof of the Zhalu Monastery. Features of the roofridge of the main hall are stone slabs with porcelain reliefs; the roof's soaring eaves are tipped with figures of animals. Chinese craftsmen are supposed to have had a share in the building of the monastery, bringing with them the glazed tiles and other materials.

199. The ruins of the first monastery of the Sakya sect, on the north bank of the Trom River. It was built in 1073, when the sect had not yet attained the sovereign position it reached later, which accounts for the relatively small scale of this monastery.

201

202

200. *The architectural style of the Sakya Monastery is based on that of Yuan dynasty castles. The square compound is surrounded by walls painted with red, black, and white stripes representing the three great Bodhisattvas Jampeyang, Chenresi, and Chanadorje. The lintels are decorated with hangings in the same colors.*

201. *Standing on the south side of the Trom River, the Sakya Monastery was built by the Sakya religious lord Phagpa, with the aid of the Yuan (Mongolian) dynasty of China. Phagpa attained both religious and political power in Tibet. This is the entrance to one of the major halls.*

202. *The resplendent main hall of the Sakya Monastery, with a ceiling that reaches 33 feet in height and forty huge columns, the thickest of them measuring 18.15 feet in diameter. The hall could seat 400 monks, and contains statues of the various Sakya religious lords.*

203

204

203. *The stupa hall in the Sakya Monastery. There are eleven stupas in the hall, containing the remains of successive religious lords of the sect, of which two are seen here.*

204. *The Tantric practices of the Kagyu-pa sect depiected in a fresco on the upper floor of the main hall of the Sakya Monastery.*

205. *"The Wealth-providing Law-protecting Master," one of the frescoes in the corridors that encircle the Sakya Monastery.*

264

207

206. *In the painted corridors of the Sakya Monastery there are 139 mandalas, or mystical cosmic diagrams, like these. All of them were painted in 1281 by the Ponchen (Great Master) Kunga Zangpo on orders from Phagpa, the all-powerful religious lord of the Sakya sect.*

207. *The Sakya Monastery in the course of construction. This fresco in the East Hall shows some of the 13,000 laborers who worked on the site.*

208. *The Sakya Monastery has a priceless collection of tens of thousands of ancient Tibetan books and manuscripts. The way the scrolls are stored gives no idea of the riches contained in them.*

209. *This robe, preserved in the Sakya Monastery, is one of countless garments that came here as gifts from emperors of the Yuan and Ming dynasties.*

210

210. One of a set of thangka scrolls recording the lives of the Sakya religious lords that were painted during the reign of Phagpa, the fifth of the line. In the center is a portrait of Khon Konchog Gyalpo, founder of the Sakya sect.

211. "The Great Debate," showing the fourth Sakya religious lord, Sakya Pandita, debating with heretical Indian scholars such as Drotan Gawa. Sakya Pandita won his case after thirteen days of intense debate, and the Indians were converted to orthodox Buddhism and even ordained as monks. Such debates were highly ritualized; the participants used dramatic and symbolic gestures to introduce and emphasize their questions and answers.

212. The Palchor Monastery at Gyantse, built between 1414 and 1424.

214

215

213. The octagonal great chorten of the Palchor Monastery has six stories, 108 doors, and a total height of 107 feet. Each floor is a separate hall for worship, with images of Buddhas. It has been claimed that there are around a hundred thousand Buddhist images in this great pagoda-like chorten, and it is therefore sometimes called "the Pagoda of the Hundred Thousand."

214. A statue of an Arhat in the Arhat Hall in the Palchor Monastery. There are twenty clay statues of Arhats, all artistic treasures dating back to the fifteenth century.

215. Statues of the great religious kings of seventh-, eight-, and ninth-century Tibet at Palchor: Songtsen Gampo, Trisong Detsen, and Ralpachen. They are carved in wood and date from the fifteenth century. The background walls are covered with splendid frescoes.

216

216. The Trashilungpo Monastery at Shigatse, founded in 1447 by the First Dalai Lama, Gedun Truppa, later became the home of successive Panchen Lamas.

217. The golden roofs of the Trashilungpo Monastery.

218. The gold-plated bronze statue of the future Buddha Maitreya (in Tibetan, Champa) in the Great Champa Hall, which is the finest building in the whole Trashilungpo Monastery. Standing 87.1 feet tall, the statue contains 6,700 taels, or 10,050 ounces, of gold (one taels equals one and a half ounces). It bears eloquent witness to the high level of bronze casting achieved by Tibetan craftsmen.

219

220

219. *Splendidly robed goddesses in the Goddess Palace next to the greater prayer hall at Trashilungpo.*

220. *The stupa of the Fourth Panchen Lama at the Trashilungpo Monastery. Begun in 1662, it took four years to complete.*

221. *The greater prayer hall is the earliest building in the Trashilungpo Monastery. Begun in 1447 but not completed until twelve years later, the entire hall has seating capacity for more than 2,000 monks.*

222

222. The Panchen Lama's throne in the Trashilungpo Monastery. Here on important religious occasions he has traditionally expounded Buddhist scriptures.

223. The bedchamber of the Panchen Lama.

224. The new palace at Shigatse, built in 1954 as a summer residence for the Panchen Lama.

223

225

225/226. *Two of the thirty-two thangkas recording the life of Sakyamuni that are preserved in the library of the Trashilungpo Monastery. The series was printed by the famous Narthang Temple Printing House in the nineteenth century.*

purely Tibetan naked goddess riding on a sow, all are works of the Tang dynasty said to have been part of the dowry brought from China to Yarlung by the Tang princess Wen Cheng.

227

228

229

231

235.

235. *The Mindruling Monastery in central Tibet, founded in 1671 by Terda Lingpa, Preceptor (teacher) of the Fifth Dalai Lama. Monks of the Nyingma-pa sect living in Kham and Amdo used to come here to study the Tibetan language, medicine, and mathematics.*

236. *Another view of the Mindruling Monastery.*

237. *The Kagyu Temple is set on a cloud-capped ridge in Yadong County and surrounded by primeval forests. Buddhist shrines are found throughout Tibet, in the remotest areas as well as in the fertile and populous river valleys.*

The Authors

Ngapo Ngawang Jigmei, the author of Chapter I, "Tibet Past and Present: An Introduction," is a distinguished authority on Tibetan affairs. He is now Chairman of the Standing Committee of the People's Congress of the Tibet Autonomous Region, and Vice Chairman of the Standing Committee of the Chinese National People's Congress.

Chapel Tsetan Phuntso, the author of Chapter III, "Customs and Rituals of the Tibetans," is a famous scholar in Tibet. He is currently Vice President of the Lhasa Committee of the Chinese People's Political Consultative Conference.

Na Zhen, the author of Chapter IV, "Women, Marriage and the Family," is a former serf. She is now President of the Women's Association of the Tibet Autonomous Region.

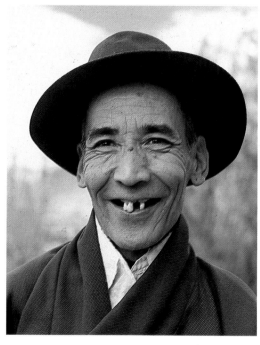

Khrili Chodra, the author of Chapter II, "The Land," is a senior editor at the Tibet People's Publishing House. He is a graduate of the Central College of National Minorities and is well versed in both the Tibetan and Chinese languages.

Dongge Luosantselie, the author of Chapter VII, "Palaces, Monasteries and Their Art," is well known as an expert on Tibetan history and culture. Formerly an Incarnation Lama, he is now an associate professor in the Beijing Central Nationalities Institute.

Jampei Chinlei, the author of Chapter VI, "Tibetan Buddhism," is a High Incarnation Lama in the Drepung Monastery of Lhasa. He is Vice Chairman of the Tibet branch of the Chinese Buddhist Association, and Vice President of the Chinese People's Political Consultative Conference.

Cai Xiansheng, the author of Chapter V, "Ethnic Minorities in Tibet," is a veteran reporter and editor for the Tibet Daily. After graduating from the department of journalism of Fudan University in Shanghai, he went to Tibet, where he has been working for the past two decades. He is our only Chinese author; all the rest are Tibetans.

Chronology

Jampei Chinlei
edited by Fosco Maraini

prehistory	Neolithic culture in Tibet.
pre-7c.	Nyatri Tsenpo becomes ruler of Yarlung tribes. Construction of the Yumbu Language.
618–842	Yarlung dynasty of Tibetan kings. (Some dates are controversial.)
618–649	Songsten Gampo. This king moves capital to Lhasa. He marries a Nepalese princess, Bhrikuti Devi, then a Chinese princess, Wen Cheng; both are instrumental in converting king and court to Buddhism.
649–676	Mangsong Mangtsen.
676–704	Dusong Mangje.
704–754	Tride Tsugtsen. This king marries the Chinese princess Jin Cheng, another fervent Buddhist.
755–797	Trisong Detsen. This king is a convinced Buddhist; calls Santarakshita, Padmasambhava, and other famous Indian masters of religion to Tibet. Building of the great monastery at Samye (about 779) and ordination of first Tibetan monks. Council of Lhasa and disputation between Chinese and Indian masters; Indian school prevails.
797–800	Muni Tsenpo.
800–815	Tride Songtsen.
815–838	Ralpachen. Peace between Tibet and Tang Dynasty of China (821).
838–842	Lang Darma. This king rejects Buddhism and supports the native Bon religion, but is murdered by a Buddhist monk; shortly afterward the Tibetan kingdom disintegrates. This period marks the end of the Earlier Spread of Buddhism. Only one Tibetan Buddhist (Lamaist) sect, the Nyingma-pa, survives from it.
9th c.	Descendants of the Tibetan kings flee to remote parts of the country and set up petty kingdoms.
10th c.–11th c.	Beginning of the Later Spread of Buddhism. Age of the great teachers—Rinchen Zangpo (Tibetan), Atisha (Indian), Marpa (Indian), Milarepa (Tibetan).
11th c.	Rise of the principal Tibetan Buddhist (Lamaist sects Kagyu-pa, Kadam-pa, and Sakya.
1027	First year of the Rabjung, the sixty-year-cycle Tibetan calendar.
1056	Drom Tonpa, a disciple of Atisha, founds the Reting Monastery north of Lhasa; beginnings of the Kadam-pa sect.
1073	Khon Konchog Gyalpo founds the first Sakya monastery; origins of the Sakya sect.
1158	Dorje Gyalpo founds the Thel Monastery near Tsethang; origins of the Phamo Drupa (Pagdru) sect.
1205	Ikhtiyar-ud-din fails in his attempt to invade Tibet from the west.
1239	Mongol forces invade Tibet.
1247	Sakya Pandita reaches an agreement with the Mongol prince Godan at Liangzhou in Gansu, northwestern China.
1264	Phagpa Lodro Gyaltsen is named Tishri (Imperial Preceptor) and invested with rule of Ü-Tsang.
1337	Muhammad Thghlug fails in his attempt to invade Tibet from the western Himalayas.
mid-14th c.	Yuan dynasty falls in China; Tibet regains de facto independence. Rise of the Phamo Drupa dynasty in Tibet; Changchub Gyaltsen (1302–1364) ruler of Ü-Tsang. Fall of the Sakya power.
1357–1419	Birth and death of Tsongkhapa, the great reformer of Lamaism and founder of the Gelug-pa ("Yellow Cap") sect, from which the Dalai Lamas are to come.
1409–1419	Founding of the three great monasteries of the Gelug-pa sect—Gandan, Drepung, and Sera.
15th c.	Rise to power in Tsang of the Rinpung clan, who favor the Karma-pa sect, an offshoot of the Kagyu-pa Rivalry with the Gelug-pa sect, a growing theocratic power in Lhasa.
1447	Gedun Truppa founds the Trashilungpo Monastery near Shigatse. He is considered by later Tibetan historians to have been the First Dalai Lama (1391–1475).
mid-16th c.	Rise of the Tsangto clan in Tsang.
1578	Sonam Gyatso (1543–1588), third pontiff of the Gelug-pa sect, given the title of Dalai Lama ("Master Ocean of Wisdom") by the Mongol prince Altan Khan, descendant of Genghis Khan.
1589–1617	Yonten Gyatso, Fourth Dalai Lama, great-grandson of Altan Khan.
1617–1682	Ngawang Lozang Gyatso, Fifth Dalai Lama ("the Great Fifth").
1642	Gushri Khan, chief of the Qoshot Mongols, defeats the Tsangto lord of Tsang, protector of the Karma-pa sect, thus establishing the full power of the Gelug-pa in Lhasa, center of the Tibetan world.
1644	Fall of the Ming Dynasty in China; rise of the Qing (Manchu) dynasty.
1652–1653	The Fifth Dalai Lama visits Beijing.
1682–1705	Sangye Gyatso regent of Tibet.
1683–1706	Sixth Dalai Lama.
1706–1720	Period of turmoil after the deposition and death of the Sixth Dalai Lama. Dzungar Mongols invade Tibet.
1716–1721	Jesuit missionaries under Father Ippolito Desideri, reside in Lhasa; Western knowledge of Tibetan culture greatly expanded.
1718–1720	Chinese intervention in Tibet; Dzungar forces expelled; Chinese occupation of Lhasa.
1728	Chinese imperial officials (Ambans) appointed to Tibet; Tibet under the suzerainty of China.
1750	Creation of the Kashag, administrative council of the Tibetan government, composed of four ministers, generally two monks and two laymen.
1757	Appointment of the Demo Trulku Jampel Delek, a high lama of the Drepung Monastery, as regent during the infancy of the Eighth Dalai Lama.
1788–1791	First Nepali-Tibetan war; Nepalese forces repulsed with the aid of Chinese imperial forces.
1841–1842	War with the rajas of Jammu and Kashmir; Tibet loses Ladakh.
1844–1846	The Lazarist fathers Huc and Gabet visit Lhasa.
1855–1856	Second Nepali-Tibetan war; Tibetans recover some border treaties. Commercial treaty with Nepal.
1890	Treaty with British regarding Sikkim.
1893	Commercial treaty between Britain and Tibet.
1904	British military expedition to Lhasa under Colonel Francis Younghusband; Lhasa briefly occupied, the Thirteenth Dalai Lama flees to Mongolia.
1904–1908	Commercial and other conventions between Tibet and the British.
1908	The Thirteenth Dalai Lama returns to Lhasa, but soon (1910) takes refuge in India because of dissension with the Chinese Amban.
1911	Republican revolution in China. Fall of the Qing dynasty. Return of the Thirteenth Dalai Lama from India; expulsion of the Chinese representatives. Tibet proclaims its independence.
1911–1951	De facto independence of Tibet.
1934	Death of the Thirteenth Dalai Lama.
1940	Installation of the Fourteenth Dalai Lama.
1951	The Chinese claim their traditional suzerainty over Tibet and return to Lhasa.
1959	Flight of the Dalai Lama to India. Tibet an autonomous region of the People's Republic of China.

History and General

Bacot, J.: *Introduction à l'histoire du Tibet.* Paris, Société Asiatique, 1962.

Bacot, J., F. W. Thomas, and C. Toussaint: *Documents de Touen-houang relatifs à l'histoire du Tibet.* Paris, Annales du Musée Guimet, vol. 51, 1940–1946.

Bell, C.: *Tibet, Past and Present.* Oxford, 1924. (Reprint, Oxford, 1968.)

Bell, C.: *Portrait of the Dalai Lama.* London, Collins, 1946.

Demiéville, P.: *Le Concile de Lhasa.* Paris, Presses Universitaires de France, 1952.

Desideri, I.: *An Account of Tibet* (edited by F. De Filippi). London, Routledge, 1937.

Fleming, P.: *Bayonets to Lhasa.* London, 1961.

Haarh, E.: *The Yar-lun Dynasty.* Copenhagen, Gad, 1969.

Karan, P. P.: *The Changing Face of Tibet: The Impact of Chinese Communist Ideology on the Landscape.* University Press of Kentucky, 1976.

Pelliot, P.: *Histoire ancienne du Tibet.* Paris, 1961.

Petech, L.: *China and Tibet in the Early Eighteenth Century.* Leyden, Brill, 1950. (Reprint, Westport, Hyperion, 1973.)

Richardson, H.: *Tibet and Its History.* Oxford, 1962.

Roerich, G. N.: *The Blue Annals of gZhon-nu-dpal.* Calcutta, 2 vols., 1949–1953. (Reprinted, New Delhi, 1976.)

Shakabpa, W. D.: *Tibet, a Political History.* Yale, 1967. (Reprint, 1973.)

Shen, T., and S. Liu: *Tibet and the Tibetans.* Stanford, 1953.

Schulemann, G.: *Geschichte der Dalai Lamas.* Leipzig, 1958.

Snellgrove, D. L. and H. Richardson: *A Cultural History of Tibet.* New York, 1968.

Stein, R. A.: *La civilisation Tibétaine.* Paris, Dunod, 1962. (English translation, *Tibetan Civilization,* London, 1972.)

Toscano: *Alla scoperta del Tibet.* Bologna, EMI, 1977.

Tucci, G.: *The Tombs of the Tibetan Kings.* Rome, 1950.

Tucci, G.: *Tibet paese delle nevi.* Novara, De Agostini, 1967. (English translation, *Tibet, the Land of Snows,* London, 1967.)

Waddell, L. A.: *Lhasa and Its Mysteries.* London, 1906.

Younghusband, F.: *India and Tibet.* London, Murray, 1910.

Religions of Tibet

Bell, C.: *The Religion of Tibet.* Oxford, 1931. (Reprint, Oxford, 1968.)

Beyer, S.: *The Cult of Tara.* Berkeley, University of California Press, 1973.

Blondeau, A. M.: *Les Religions du Tibet,* in H. C. Puech, *Histoire des religions.* Paris, Gallimard, 1970. (Italian translation, *Storia delle religioni,* Bari, Laterza, 1978.)

Grunwedel, A.: *Mythologie des Buddhismus in Tibet und der Mongolei.* Leipzig, 1900. (Reprint, Osnabruck, 1970.)

Guenther, H. V.: *The Jewel Ornament of Liberation by Gam-po-pa.* London, 1959.

Guenther, H. V.: *The Life and Teaching of Naropa.* Oxford, 1963.

Hoffmann, H.: *The Religions of Tibet.* London, Allen and Unwin, 1961.

Lalou, M.: *Les Religions du Tibet.* Paris, 1957.

Nebesky-Wojkowitz, R. de: *Oracles and Demons of Tibet.* Oxford, 1956.

Obermiller, E.: *History of Buddhism, by Bu-ston.* Heidelberg, 1931. (Reprint, Tokyo, 1964.)

Snellgrove, D. L.: *Buddhist Himalaya.* Oxford, 1960.

Snellgrove, D. L.: *The Hevajra Tantra.* Oxford, 2 vols., 1961.

Snellgrove, D. L.: *Himalayan Pilgrimage.* Oxford, 1961.

Snellgrove, D. L.: *Nine Ways of Bon.* London, 1967.

Snellgrove, D. L.: *Four Lamas of Dolpo.* Oxford, 1967–1968.

Tucci, G.: *Buddhism, Encyclopaedia Britannica,* 15th edition, vol. 3, pp. 374–403, 1974.

Tucci, G.: *Teoria e pratica del Mandala.* Rome, 1949. (English translation, *The Theory and Practice of Mandala,* London, Rider, 1961, and later reprints.)

Tucci, G.: *Le religioni del Tibet.* Roma, Mediterranee, 1970.

Tucci, G., and W. Heissig: *Die Religionen Tibets und der Mongolei.* Stuttgart, Kohlhammer, 1970. (French translation, *Les religions du Tibet et de la Mongolie,* Paris, Payot, 1973.)

Waddell, L. A.: *The Buddhism of Tibet or Lamaism.* London, 1893. (Reprinted, 1959.)

Art and Iconography

Bhattacharyya, B: *The Indian Buddhist Iconography.* Calcutta, Mukhopadhyay, 1968.

Clark, W. E.: *Two Lamaist Pantheons.* Cambridge, Mass., Harvard, 2 vols., 1937.

De Mallmann, M. T.: *Introduction à l'iconographie du Tântrisme Bouddhique.* Paris, Adrien-Maisonneuve, 1975.

Getty, A.: *The Gods of Northern Buddhism.* Oxford, 1928. (Reprint, Tokyo, Tuttle, 1962.)

Gordon, A. K.: *The Iconography of Tibetan Lamaism.* New York, Columbia, 1939. (Reprint, Tokyo, Tuttle, 1959.)

Gordon, A. K.: *Tibetan Religious Art.* New York, Columbia, 1952. (Reprint, Paragon, 1963.)

Karmay, H.: *Early Sino-Tibetan Art.* Warminster, Aris and Phillips, 1975.

Lauf, D. I.: *Tibetan Sacred Art.* Berkeley and London, Shambhala, 1976.

Olschak, B. C.: *Religion und Kunst im alten Tibet.* Zurich, 1962.

Olson, E.: *Catalogue of the Tibetan Collections . . . in the Newark Museum,* vols. I–V. Newark, 1950 and following years.

Pal, P.: *The Art of Tibet.* New York, 1969.

Pal, P.: *Lamaist Art: The Aesthetics of Harmony.* Boston, 1970.

Pott, P. H.: *Introduction to the Tibetan Collection of the National Museum of Ethnology, Leyden.* Leyden, 1951.

Roerich, G.: *Tibetan Paintings.* Pans, Geuthner, 1925.

Schmid, T.: *The Cotton-clad Mila.* Stockholm, 1952.

Schmid, T.: *The Eighty-five Siddhas.* Stockholm, 1958.

Seckel, D.: *Kunst der Buddhismus.* Baden-Baden, 1962. (Italian translation, *Il Buddhismo,* Milan, Saggiatore, 1963.)

Sierksma, F.: *Tibet's Terrifying Deities.* The Hague, Mouton, 1966.

Singh, M.: *Himalayan Art.* London, Macmillan, 1968. (Italian translation, *Arte Himalayana,* Milan, Electa, 1968.)

Tucci, G.: *Indo-Tibetica.* Rome, parts I–IV, 7 vols., 1932–1941.

Tucci, G.: *Tibetan Painted Scrolls.* Rome, Libreria dello Stato, 3 vols., 1949.

Various Authors: *Dieux et démons de l'Himalaya: Art du Bouddhisme Lamaique.* Catalogue of Grand Palais Exhibition, Paris, 1977.

Literature and Translations

Bacot, J.: *Trois mystères tibètains: Tchrimekunden, Djroazanmo, Nansal.* Paris, Bossard, 1921.

Bacot, J.: *Le poète tibétain Milarèpa.* Paris, Bossard, 1925.

Bacot, J.: *La conversion du chasseur,* in *Etudes d'orientalisme publièes . . . à la mémoire de R. Linossier,* vol. I. Paris, Leroux, 1932.

Bacot, J.: *La vie de marpa, la "Traducteur."* Paris, Bouddhica, I/VII, 1937.

Bacot, J.: *Zugiñima.* Paris, Cahiers de la Société Asiatique, XIV, 1957.

Chang, G. C. C.: *The Hundred Thousand Songs of Milarepa.* Boulder, Colo. Shambala, 2 vols., 1962.

Evans-Wentz, W. J.: *The Tibetan Book of the Dead.* Oxford, 1927. (Many reprints.)

Evans-Wentz, W. J.: *Tibet's great Yogi Milarepa: A biography from the Tibetan.* Oxford, 1928. (Many reprints.)

Evans-Wentz, W. J.: *Tibetan Yoga and Secret Doctrines.* Oxford, 1935.

Evans-Wentz, W. J.: *The Tibetan Book of the Great Liberation.* London, 1954.

Ferrari, A.: *Mk'yen brtse's Guide to the Holy Places of Central Tibet.* Rome, Serie Orientale Roma XVI, 1958.

Gordon, A. K.: *Tibetan Tales.* London, 1953.

Lalou, M.: *Letteratura Tibetana,* in *Storia delle letterature d'Oriente,* vol. IV, Milan, Vallardi, 1969.

Laufer, B.: *Der Roman einer Tibetischen Konigin.* Leipzig, 1911.

Stein, R. A.: *L'épopée tibétaine de Gesar dans sa version lamaique de Ling.* Paris, Presses Universitaires de France, 1956.

Toussaint, G. C.: *Le Dict de Padma (Padma Than-yig).* Paris, Hautes Etudes Chinoises, III, 1933. (English translation, *The Life and Liberation of Padmasambhava.* Emeryville, Calif., Dharma, 2 vols., 1978.)

Tucci, G.: *Il libro tibetano dei morti.* Milan, Bocca, 1949.

Tucci, G.: *Tibetan Folksongs.* Ascona, Artibus Asiae, 1949. (Second edition, 1966.)

Tucci, G.: *Letteratura Tibetana,* in *Le civiltà dell'Oriente,* Rome, Casini, 1957.

Vostrikov, A. I.: *Tibetan Historical Literature.* Calcutta, Indian Studies, 1970.

Yu, D.: *Love Songs of the Sixth Dalai Lama.* Beijing, Academia Sinica Monographs, A/5, 1930.

Travel, Exploration, Ethnology

Bacot, J.: *Le Tibet Révolté.* Paris, Hachette, 1912.
Bailey, F. M.: *No Passport to Tibet.* London, 1957.
Bell, C.: *The People of Tibet.* Oxford, Clarendon Press, 1928. (Reprint, 1968.)
Chapman, F. S.: *Lhasa, the Holy City.* London, Chatto & Windus, 1938.
Dalai Lama, XIVth: *My Land and My People.* London, 1962.
Das, S. C.: *Journey to Lhasa and Central Tibet* (1904). (Reprint, New Delhi, Manjusri, 1970.)
David-Neel, A.: *Voyage d'une parisienne à Lhassa.* Paris, Plon, 1927.
David-Neel, A.: *Mystiques et magiciens du Tibet.* Paris, Plon, 1929. (Reprint, 1973.)
David-Neel, A.: *Le journal de voyage* (1918–1940). Paris, Plon, 1976.
Duncan, M. H.: *Harvest Festival Dramas of Tibet.* Hong Kong, Orient, 1955.
Duncan, M. H.: *Customs and Superstitions of Tibetans.* London, Mitre, 1964.
Ekvall, R. B.: *Religious Observances in Tibet: Patterns and Function.* Chicago, 1964.
Gelder, S. and R.: *The Timely Rain: Travels in New Tibet.* London, Hutchinson, 1964.
Han, S.: *Lhassa, étoile-fleur.* Paris, Stock, 1976.
Harrer, H.: *Seven Years in Tibet.* New York, Dutton, 1954.
Harer, H.: *Tibet Is My Country: The Autobiography of Thubten Norbu, Brother of the Dalai Lama, as told to H. Harrer.* London, Hart-Davis, 1960.
Hedin, S.: *Trans-Himalaya.* London, 1909–1913.
Kawaguchi, E.: *Three Years in Tibet.* Madras, 1909.
Kingdon Ward, F.: *The Land of the Blue Poppy.* London, 1913 (Reprint, 1973.)
Kingdon Ward, F.: *Plant Hunting on the Edge of the World.* London, 1930. (Reprint, 1974.)
Kingdon Ward, F.: *A Plant Hunter in Tibet.* London, Cape, 1937.
Landon, P.: *Lhasa.* London, Hurst and Blackett, 2 vols., 1905.
MacDonald, D.: *The Land of the Lama.* London, 1928.
Maraini, F.: *Secret Tibet.* London, Hutchinson, 1952.
Migot, A.: *Tibetan Marches.* London, 1955.
Pallis, M.: *Peaks and Lamas.* London Cassell, 1948.
Pallis, M.: *The Way and the Mountain.* London, P. Owen, 1960.
Pemba, T.: *Young Days in Tibet.* London, Cape, 1957.
Swami Pranavananda: *Exploration in Tibet.* University of Calcutta, 1950.
Teichman, E.: *Travels of a Consular Officer in Eastern Tibet.* Cambridge, 1921.
Tucci, G.: *Cronaca della missione scientifica Tucci nel Tibet occidentale* (1933). Rome, Reale Accademia d'Italia, 1934.
Tucci, G.: *Santi e briganti nel Tibet ignoto.* Milan, Hoepli, 1937. (Reprint, Milan, 1981.)
Tucci, G.: *A Lhasa e oltre.* Rome, Libreria dello Stato, 1952.

Various

Avedon, John F.: "Exploring the Oysteries of Tibetan Medicine," *Tibet Today,* March 1981.
Rechung Rinpoche: *Tibetan Medicine.* London, Wellcome Institute, 1973.
Vandor, I.: *Bouddhisme Tibetain: Les Traditions musicales.* Paris, Buchet-Chastel, 1976.
Taring, R. D.: *Daughter of Tibet.* London, John Murray Publishers, 1970.

Records of Tibetan Music

The Music of Tibetan Buddhism (UNESCO, Musical Anthology of the Orient, nos. 9, 10, 11). Kassel, Bärenreiter-Musicaphon 30/L 2009, 2010, 2011.